WITHDRAWN

D1373871

Cooperation for Better Student Teaching

William A. Bennie
Director of Student Teaching
The University of Texas
Austin, Texas

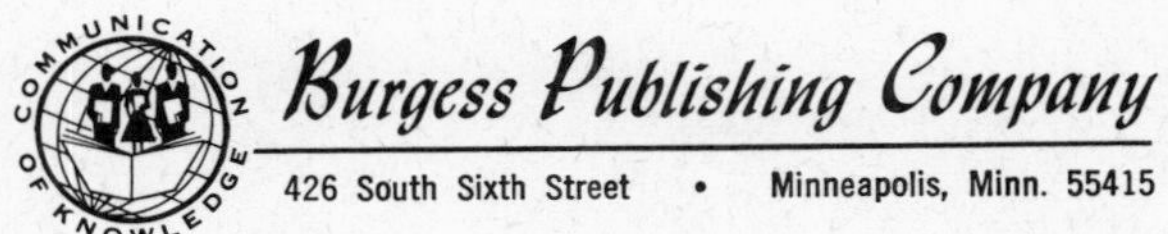

Burgess

EDUCATION SERIES

Consulting Editor — LAURENCE S. FLAUM

COOPERATION FOR BETTER STUDENT TEACHING . . . . Bennie

GUIDANCE: A LONGITUDINAL APPROACH . . . . Blanchard, Flaum

TECHNIQUES FOR TEACHING CONSERVATION EDUCATION . . . . Brown, Mouser

CREDO FOR AMERICAN PUBLIC EDUCATION . . . . Flaum

AN ECOLOGICAL APPROACH TO CONSERVATION . . . . Hamm, Nason

THE BEGINNING KINDERGARTEN TEACHER . . . . Salot, Leavitt

PHOTOSITUATIONS: A TECHNIQUE FOR TEACHING . . . . Potter, Moss, Smith

INTEGRATING OUTDOOR AND CONSERVATION EDUCATION INTO THE CURRICULUM . . . . Stapp

INVESTIGATIONS IN PHYSICAL SCIENCE . . . . Strickland

---

Printed in the United States of America

Library of Congress Catalog Card Number 66-19902

Preface

The increasing use of public schools as laboratories for the student teaching experience has demanded new insights into the operation of student teaching programs for both college and public school personnel. Both groups must have mutually accepted understandings concerning the role of student teaching, the expectations of the experience, and the operational procedures involved.

No rigid prescription may be made to insure success in student teaching; however, there are basic principles and accepted practices which appear to foster better experiences. Although somewhat idealistic in places, this text attempts to take a realistic look at student teaching and to suggest some principles which should be incorporated into most college programs.

This effort is aimed at public school administrators and teachers who participate in student teaching programs and at college administrators and supervisors who are also involved. Its intent is to improve the quality of student teaching through improved cooperation.

The author is indebted to those publishers who granted permission to reproduce excerpts from materials and to those many student teachers, classroom teachers, and college supervisors with whom he has worked for many years. A special acknowledgement is due his wife, Betty, whose patience and understanding as a sounding-board for the ideas contained herein contributed greatly to their eventual evolvement.

William A. Bennie

Austin, Texas

Table of Contents

Chapter I

Student Teaching – Its Nature and Nurture

The role of student teaching in the preparation of teachers is more significant today than at any time since the certification of teachers became accepted practice. The critical reappraisal of education in general and teacher education in particular which drew considerable attention during the 1950's and which still exists to some extent today has, if anything, added to the already important role of the student teaching experience. It is undoubtedly the most common element of teacher education, and, if those who have undergone the experience are to be believed, is the most valuable of the pre-service professional courses.

It is significant that the most vociferous critics of professional education have usually spared student teaching from their criticisms or have at least treated it kindly. Indeed, such reputable commentators on American education as Conant[1] enthusiastically endorse this aspect of teacher education. This is probably due to the satisfaction expressed by teachers who have included student teaching in their own preparation as well as the inherent value of practical experience which has long been accepted as a worthwhile way of learning.

The role of student teaching has changed considerably in recent years. Although it has long been a basic aspect of teacher education, for many years the student teaching experience was considered in somewhat the same context as any other professional course in the teacher education curriculum. The one-hour-per-day pattern was the common one which occasionally found several student teachers assigned to the same class. As the values of the course began to assert themselves, provision for the experience was expanded and enlarged upon with longer and larger blocks of time included until now the course incorporates a substantial teaching experience in many cases. Programs requiring a full day of student teaching

[1] James B. Conant, The Education of American Teachers, New York: McGraw Hill Book Company, 1963.

for a full semester are not uncommon; and, in some instances, newer programs of internship go further than this to a considerable extent. The fact that this change has come about in the face of a general reduction of total professional hours is, in itself, a significant indication of the relative value placed on the actual teaching experience found in the student teaching program. As one reflects on the changing pattern of student teaching throughout the years, it is obvious that the program has come far since 1722 when one John Campbell apprenticed himself to one George Brownell to "learn the art, trade, and mystery of teaching."

What is student teaching?

If this question had been asked a few years ago, the reply would surely have been, "this is the time when the prospective teacher practices what he has been taught. Here he applies the theory he has learned in his Education courses." The experience would have been undertaken under the close scrutiny of a "critic" teacher whose very title was frightening.

Today, student teaching is regarded as another step in a logical sequence of professional courses. The change in course title from *practice teaching* to *student teaching* indicates a changed philosophy. The student teacher is considered to be engaged in a learning situation--a *student* of *teaching*. No longer does he "practice" what he has been taught, but he is encouraged to experiment, to probe, to inquire, and to learn for himself how the theory previously studied applies to real pupils in actual classrooms. The classroom has become a laboratory where the prospective teacher attempts to synthesize the theory he has studied with the experience of teaching into a more complete understanding of teaching and learning. Teaching theory is extended into the classroom for refinement and integration into a workable philosophy of teaching. This is done with the watchful and helpful assistance of the cooperating teacher in whose classroom the student teacher is experiencing his first teaching assignments.

Closely involved in the overall experience is the college supervisor whose job it is to work closely with both student teacher and cooperating teacher in making the student teaching experience as rewarding and rich as possible. The college supervisor, which has recently evolved as a distinct professional role in itself, serves in a liaison capacity between the college which is preparing teachers and the public schools which are providing the framework, the laboratory, and much of the instruction in the student teaching course.

This newer concept of student teaching recognizes that the college student does not learn all about how to teach in this relatively short exposure to the classroom. It is realized that the development of a master teacher is a process involving several years of successful teaching and further study. Supervisory programs, in-service education, graduate courses, and many professional journals all attest to this constant striving for improvement by teachers. It is hoped, however, that through his student teaching experience, the prospective teacher will become sufficiently familiar with the teaching role that he can do a creditable job during his initial years of teaching and will develop a readiness to profit from that experience to the point where he can become the kind of teacher which is desirable in today's complex society.

This concept of student teaching, if accepted by the public schools, imposes the responsibility of in-service supervision on the schools whereby the student teaching objectives are extended into the early years of classroom teaching. Many public schools have recognized this and have built orientation programs for beginning teachers with such a goal in mind.

In the definition of student teaching accepted by the Association for Student Teaching and which is usually found in the professional literature, the experience is described as "the period of guided teaching when the student takes increasing responsibility for the work with a given group of learners over a period of consecutive weeks." It should be noted that this definition refers to *guided teaching, increasing responsibility*, and *consecutive weeks*. Guided teaching implies that supervisory help must be provided; increasing responsibility indicates the gradual induction of the student to the teaching role; and consecutive weeks refers to the need for a continual period of teaching to the point where the student teacher realizes the need for continuity in teaching and where he can see the effects of his teaching. In subsequent chapters these aspects of the experience will be elaborated upon as the responsibilities of those charged with the implementation of the student teaching course are outlined and explained.

The setting for student teaching

As one might expect, the growth of student teaching paralleled quite closely the gradual improvement of teacher education and certification. There were early programs of student teaching scattered among a few of the better normal schools in the latter half of the nineteenth century which endeavored to provide laboratory experiences to aspiring teacher candidates. As the normal schools gave way to teachers colleges and the four-year preparation program began to make progress, student teaching came into its own as an integral part of the educational process for teachers. The beginning of The Association for Student Teaching in 1920 gives an indication of the status of the field by that date.

As state universities began providing teacher education and teachers colleges grew to reasonable size, the laboratory school made its bow in order that the student teaching experience could be provided by the teacher education institutions in situations reflecting the prevailing theories of teaching and learning. Although there has been some utilization of the public schools in student teaching for many years, it was only during the past two decades that they have been called upon to provide the major resource for this practical experience of teaching, except for the occasional programs of smaller institutions who could not afford to build and maintain a campus school or whose involvement in teacher education was not a major commitment.

The laboratory school has been both lauded and condemned. It was often criticized as not being "realistic" and "practical" for teacher education. Pupils were often atypical, resources were more abundant than in many public schools, and class size and teacher loads were often of optimum proportion.

While there is some element of truth in these accusations, the experiences provided by the laboratory schools were not as bad as often pictured. Here the prospective teachers were introduced to teaching in a carefully planned and controlled situation. The teachers with whom they worked were often indeed master teachers who had the time and materials to do the job of teaching with maximum efficiency and competency. Often the supervising teachers had special preparation to do the job of working with student teachers and were given teaching loads compatible with the additional supervisory duties which were expected of them. In this atmosphere the student teacher could not help but develop concepts of teaching which, although idealistic, gave him something to work toward. To borrow a phrase, his reach often exceeded his grasp.

The enrollment explosion of the forties, however, demanded a corresponding increase in teachers. This, coupled with the desire for longer and more extensive teaching experiences, made the campus school obviously inadequate--hence, the inclusion of the public school in the teacher education picture to a point never before imagined. Another important consideration which led to this end was the relatedness of the public school student teaching experience to the actual teaching situation normally assumed by beginning teachers. This movement to the public schools left the campus laboratory school in a state of momentary confusion as it sought to find itself in the new scheme of things. Lately, laboratory schools have become identified with experimentation and research and as likely sources of additional laboratory experiences for prospective teachers.

Today, literally hundreds of public schools find themselves the center of active teacher education. Teachers and administrators suddenly find themselves thrust into an active role for which they have no special preparation and little or no assistance in adjusting to it. By now, the increased utilization of the public schools in student teaching has reached the point where the quantitative aspects of the student teaching experience are accepted but where many persons, both in colleges and in the public schools, are raising questions concerning the aspects of a quality program.

Student teaching programs as they operate today are neither the sole responsibility of the public schools nor of the teacher education institutions. Since the course is still a college offering with accompanying credit, the college or university bears the ultimate responsibility for the granting of credit and, usually, the final grade in student teaching if a grade is given. The actual implementation of the course, however, is a joint responsibility. Public schools provide the laboratory, the pupils, the cooperating teacher, and the attendant facilities in guiding the student teacher. The college provides the student teacher, the pre-student teaching professional courses, and the supervision to assist the cooperating teacher and the student teacher in reaching the objectives of the student teaching course.

The use of the public schools in student teaching opens wide a myriad of possibilities for laboratory experiences. The laboratory itself includes the school building, the school community, and the school district which offer widespread opportunities to learn not only the intensive approaches to classroom teaching but also the extensive implications inherent in the overall educational process. This then is the setting in which student teaching currently operates--the possibilities are endless; the challenge is indeed great.

Within this setting, patterns of student teaching of various kinds may be found. It is impossible to identify any specific pattern which might be called ideal; these change considerably from institution to institution and even within an institution. All contribute to the same general objectives however. Programs may be found which range from a few hours per day to a full day in student teaching and from a few weeks to an entire semester or even longer. The nature of the pattern is important for it indicates the pacing of the student teaching experience and the emphasis for the course. Obviously, the longer the prospective teacher is in the classroom, the more opportunities he will have to participate in the various functions of the teaching role, increasing his understanding and skill. This does identify an area, however, in which teacher education needs to do considerable research--determining the student teaching pattern which seemingly does the best job of preparing teachers.

The movement of student teaching into the public schools was not done without accompanying problems to the colleges involved. A survey of 282 institutions, conducted by The Association for Student Teaching in 1959, revealed several problems encountered by colleges in establishing off-campus student teaching programs.[2] Among the problems were the following, listed in order of frequency of mention:

1. Providing for in-service training of supervising teachers in cooperating schools.
2. Identifying and recruiting competent supervising teachers in cooperating schools.
3. Developing understanding on the part of supervising teachers of procedures and policies of the college relating to the student teaching experience.

[2] Charles M. Clarke, Editor, Teacher Education and the Public Schools, 40th Yearbook, The Association for Student Teaching, 1961, pp. 141-163.

4. Determining the load of college supervisors.
5. Revising curriculum patterns and course scheduling in the Education Department.
6. Revising curriculum patterns and course scheduling in departments other than Education.
7. Involving supervising teachers and administrators in cooperating schools in the development and evaluation of the off-campus student teaching program.
8. Arranging with college dormitory officials for the time students are away from campus.
9. Recruiting personnel to serve as college supervisors.
10. Establishing policies relating to the participation of students in college extra-curricular activities.
11. Determining the most desirable length of student teaching assignments.
12. Providing in-service training for college supervisors.
13. Providing funds for payment to supervising teachers, school administrators, and/or cooperating school districts.
14. Arranging housing for students while they are student teaching off-campus.

It is perhaps worthy of mention that the three most frequently-mentioned problems were concerned with the identification and preparation of classroom teachers to serve as cooperating teachers. Because of the great importance of this job, there is much sensitivity on the part of the college to recruiting competent teachers for assuming this responsibility. The size of the student teaching population, often concentrated in one area; the rate of teacher turnover; and the ever-changing complexities of the teaching role are all factors contributing to the scarcity of competent cooperating teachers. This one area still remains one of the greatest problems in the student teaching field and poses implications for the in-service preparation of those teachers who are available.

It is also recognized that student teaching creates additional problems for the public schools since it places still another responsibility on the already crowded doorstep of public education. These include creating opportunities for the student teacher to explore the many facets of teaching, providing instructional experiences while still maintaining the quality of classroom instruction, finding time for the necessary conferences and planning required, as well as assisting in the identification of competent supervising teachers. The values of student teaching, however, in improving the quality of classroom teachers are worth the effort made to solve the problems which they bring.

The student teaching assignment

The most critical aspect of the student teaching experience and the most important element in the success or failure of any student teacher is the specific assignment provided him. The assignment includes many factors. The best student teaching experiences occur when the assignment has been very carefully made--where the abilities of the cooperating teacher have been carefully matched with the unique talents of the student teacher. Many things need to be considered--the teaching fields, the personality of each party, the student teacher's academic ability, the socio-economic level of the pupils, the attitude of the student teacher and the cooperating teacher, the competency of the cooperating teacher, and the willingness of the school administration to accept and work with the student teacher to be assigned.

Procedures for the assignment of student teachers vary widely from college to college; however, it is generally considered that the best assignment stems from the joint efforts of the college supervisor and the building principal whose experiences in the past have acquainted them with the school and with specific teachers. Generally, final approval for assignments is given by the college Director of Student Teaching and the corresponding official in the administrative offices of the public school.

There are many questions which must be resolved before the final assignment of a student teacher may be made. Many of these involve the crystallization of a philosophy of student teaching which must be accepted by both public schools and colleges. These involve questions concerning the assignment of student teachers in situations where elementary grades are departmentalized, where ability grouping is used, where all-level teaching fields are involved.

Decisions must also be made as to whether or not a student teacher should teach in more than one teaching field, if one or more cooperating teachers are to be used with each student teacher, if different grade levels are to be incorporated into the teaching experience. While various institutions have differing points of view concerning these many problems, it is generally thought that student teachers perform best in normal or near-normal situations with enrichment experiences supplementing these in deviant classes or in other teaching fields or grade levels. Consensus on these many problems, however, must be reached before plans may be made incorporating the decisions into specific assignments.

If the cooperating teacher has had previous experiences with student teachers, there will be some evidence of the teacher's proficiency in the role of cooperating teacher. If the teacher is new to the role, however, care must be taken to insure that his selection for the job is a wise one. Since only experienced teachers should be used, the building principal should have some basis for decision from his experience with the teacher. In this way the element of chance is curtailed to some extent.

One of the biggest problems in the placement of student teachers is the lack of sufficient knowledge about the student teacher to enable those who are making the assignment to use their best judgment. Each semester brings a new group of students from the college classrooms into student teaching with the college supervisor often knowing little about them as individuals. As teacher education institutions become larger and larger, this problem may become magnified since professor-student contacts are often lessened and personal relationships more difficult to maintain. Certain facts about prospective teachers may be ascertained from assessment instruments of various kinds; however, the important personal knowledge of unique talents and abilities and acquaintance with personality factors of student teachers remain unknown in many instances.

This is an internal problem which teacher education institutions must resolve if they are to do their share in securing proper placement assignments for student teachers. There can be no doubt but that the proper placement, which can make or break a teacher of the future, must be made through securing as much information as possible about all parties concerned.

The student teacher's preparation

An examination of the professional curricula of various institutions reveals a disparaging array of professional courses taken by student teachers before the student teaching level is reached. To the uninitiated, it appears that there is little common agreement as to what should constitute the pattern of courses and content in the education of teachers. Closer scrutiny of the content of the courses, however, discloses somewhat general similarities. The sequence of the content does vary on occasion.

Much criticism of the excessive amount of professional education claimed for prospective teachers has been voiced in the past which has resulted in a general reduction of the number of professional courses required. In most institutions at present the professional curriculum has been pared to essential elements which can be satisfactorily defended.

Regardless of the specific course sequence, prospective teachers come to student teaching with certain theoretical acquaintance with teaching. Normally, the student will have some understanding of the American school system and the issues and trends attendant thereto. He will have some psychological understanding of boys and girls and the causes of behavior as well as basic instruction in sound principles of teaching. He will have an acquaintance with some materials for teaching in his particular areas and will have been introduced to the basic ingredients of lesson planning.

In practice, most of this professional study will have been at the theoretical level involving little contact with the classroom; however, there is a decided trend toward including more opportunities for observation of both pupils and teachers and active participation in the learning situation to make the theoretical study more realistic. Good programs of teacher education go far in this direction; however, the limitations of numbers, time, and availability of opportunities for desirable observation and participation by college students often restrict pre-student teaching laboratory experiences considerably.

The student teacher usually has a basic foundation of general education. While specific hours vary, the amount of foundation studies centers around sixty semester hours or approximately two years of college. Naturally, definition of what constitutes general education is involved and may be interpreted differently in different institutions, thereby creating much of the disparity in the number of credit hours. In addition, prospective secondary teachers may be expected to have some depth in one or two specialized areas by the time student teaching is reached. Academic strength in the teaching field varies considerably, perhaps from 15 to 30 semester hours, depending upon the field involved and certification requirements.

Elementary student teachers normally will have enriched the general education requirements with additional courses in areas commonly found in the elementary classroom--geography, art, music, science, mathematics, etc. There has been a trend to include some depth in preparation in at least one academic field for prospective elementary teachers as well as a decided movement to increase the amount of general education for all prospective teachers.

The organization of student teaching

Student teaching has been the capstone course of the professional curriculum traditionally. In the great majority of schools it is offered in the senior year of college with a few institutions permitting some students to enroll as juniors if they have the necessary prerequisites.

There are some professional educators who feel that the student teaching experience should be taken earlier in order that some of the professional courses might follow it. It is felt that such a program makes the theoretical courses more valuable since the college students have concrete classroom experience upon which their theoretical study may be based. Considerable speculation could be made as to whether student teaching is an inductive or deductive experience.

Woodruff[3] reported that there is a growing body of opinion in favor of earlier student teaching with as much of the theoretical study as possible coming after the experience.

In spite of this, however, he also reported that a study of teacher preparation institutions in 1959 indicated the principal value of student teaching as being to bring all aspects of teaching into integration. Next in importance was the development

[3] Asahel D. Woodruff, Student Teaching Today, Study Series No. 5, The American Association of Colleges for Teacher Education, Washington, D.C., 1960, p. 3.

of skill in teaching.[4] It would appear from this that the majority of educators favor student teaching late in the professional program. One might also assume that these values can best be reached by a full-time student teaching experience since at least one of these values, bringing all aspects of teaching into integration, necessitates familiarization with the overall teaching role. The same study, however, also reported that the most frequent pattern of student teaching was the half-day assignment. Nearly equal in number, however, were the institutions with full-time student teaching experiences provided for their prospective teachers.

Objectives of student teaching

Although each student teaching experience is unique, there are many areas in which all student teachers should gain various degrees of competency. Some of these are quite obvious; others are less so. While it is impossible to list all the outcomes which are gained by all student teachers, some of them are so common that they may be identified.

During student teaching the prospective teacher gains a much wider understanding of boys and girls. Even though the student teacher himself is often not much older than some of the pupils in his class, particularly at the secondary level, he looks at them from a different perspective as he plans how to reach them as a teacher. He gains knowledge about their interests, their attitudes toward school and toward one another, their reactions to various stimuli, their home backgrounds, as well as a considerable knowledge of their social, emotional, mental, and physical development. This is an outcome which is inevitable if the student teacher takes advantage of his many opportunities to discover more about learners and how they learn. Among the kinds of specific activities in which the student teacher may engage which will lead to the attainment of this objective are:

1. Holding individual conferences with pupils
2. Making a case study of pupil or pupils
3. Observing activities of pupils in many situations
4. Studying cumulative records

[4] Ibid., p. 31.

5. Directing study hall, lunchroom, library, and playground activities
6. Holding conferences with other teachers and guidance personnel
7. Working with slow learners and gifted learners
8. Working with small groups of pupils
9. Attending school social affairs
10. Doing actual teaching in the classroom

Another outcome which should evolve from the student teaching experience is the promotion of the proper educational climate in the classroom. This includes the creation and maintenance of a healthful, democratic, workable environment. Contributing to this end are the following experiences for the student teacher:

1. Having responsibilities concerning light, heat, and ventilation
2. Arranging seating of pupils
3. Participating in pupil-teacher planning
4. Arranging display materials
5. Observing the cooperating teacher at work
6. Handling minor discipline problems
7. Preparing bulletin boards

By the completion of the student teaching experience, prospective teachers should have had the opportunity to select, organize, and present classroom teaching materials. This involves:

1. Planning and teaching a unit(s) of work
2. Providing for individual differences among pupils
3. Providing for and guiding classroom discussion
4. Screening current materials for use in daily plans
5. Having conferences with the cooperating teacher concerning the on-going activities of the class
6. Having conferences with the college supervisor
7. Observing many different teachers in actual teaching situations
8. Doing actual teaching using various approaches
9. Evaluating critically the progress of the class
10. Experimenting with methods and materials
11. Learning to use audio-visual materials and equipment

Another outcome of student teaching which adds to the security of the beginning teacher and which paves the way for further development as a classroom teacher is the familiarization which the student teacher gets with the total role of the teacher, including the many routine duties expected of him. These include:

1. Recording and submitting attendance data
2. Making anecdotal references
3. Attending faculty and PTA meetings
4. Accepting extra assignments in study halls, lunchroom, etc.
5. Helping make out grade reports
6. Scheduling movies, requisitioning supplies, etc.
7. Keeping routine daily records
8. Assisting with parent conferences
9. Participating in the supervision of extra-curricular activities

During student teaching, the prospective teacher becomes acquainted with the problems and importance of collecting, interpreting, and using data in the evaluation of pupil growth. In order to achieve this outcome, student teachers should engage in:

1. Preparing and administering tests
2. Scoring and grading examinations
3. Becoming familiar with standardized tests
4. Determining grades at terminal grading points
5. Keeping daily records
6. Holding conferences with pupils and parents
7. Utilizing cumulative records of pupils

Another particularly valuable outgrowth of student teaching is the attainment of self-confidence and poise which the prospective teacher gains. Here for the first time, teaching is a *real* thing, not something on the far horizon which he will meet some day in the future. Here for the first time the student has the *feeling* of being a teacher. This is a tremendously stimulating experience for the future teacher, for this is the beginning of a true professional attitude. All of the activities in which the student participates aid in the attainment of this outcome. Nothing succeeds like success and student teaching is no exception. Nothing is more valuable than this one area in paving the way for future growth and improvement--the knowledge that one is a professional and is capable of doing a professional job.

In summary, these outcomes might be listed as objectives for student teachers and those who work with them to keep constantly in mind as the student teaching experience unfolds:

1. The student teacher should develop deeper insights and understandings of the mental, emotional, social, and physical development of boys and girls.
2. The student teacher should learn how to select, organize, and present classroom work in a variety of ways.
3. The student teacher should learn how to develop and maintain a healthful, democratic, workable environment in the classroom.
4. The student teacher should become familiar with the total role of the teacher in and out of the classroom.
5. The student teacher should learn how to collect, interpret, and use data in the evaluation of pupil and group growth.
6. The student teacher should develop self-confidence to the point where he can do a creditable job of teaching.

There are undoubtedly other outgrowths of student teaching which could be added to the above, but these are indicative of the elements in which the student teacher needs to reach a level of competency for satisfactory performance in the classroom.

A point of view

The concept of student teaching as reflected in this and subsequent chapters is based on a point of view which is generally consistent with the trends and procedures endorsed by persons active in the student teaching field. The point of view involved embraces the following tenets:

1. Student teaching is a desirable aspect of teacher education. While there are undoubtedly some individuals who could perform satisfactorily in the classroom without the student teaching experience, there are hundreds of others whose transformation from college student to classroom teacher is smoother, easier, and more educationally profitable by having undergone their first teaching experience under the guidance offered in student teaching.

2. Student teaching is a joint responsibility of public schools and academic and professional divisions of teacher

education institutions. Teachers cannot be educated in a vacuum nor can they be educated in isolation from the classroom. The total responsibility for the preparation of high quality teachers is shared by those who employ them as well as those who provide for their formal education, including academic and professional departments of institutions of higher education. Knowledge and method go hand in hand.

3. Each student teaching experience must be considered as a unique situation. While there are many common elements in a satisfactory student teaching assignment, as reflected throughout these pages, these must be adjusted to conform to specific personalities, schools, subjects, and procedures. The fact that teachers differ from one another is a distinct strength of education.

4. Student teaching is a developmental process through which the college student moves as he grows professionally and personally. The psychological concept of moving from simple to complex to more complex responsibilities should be the underlying principle in providing student teaching experiences. The student teacher moves at his own rate.

5. Planning is the main ingredient of the formula for successful student teaching. Planning for the development of the student teacher as a professional person and planning by the participants for effective teaching are both essential. There is a direct relationship between the amount of planning involved by all parties and the benefits derived by the student teacher from his experiences.

6. Student teaching is an educational process involving the acquisition of insights, understandings, and skills, each of which is interrelated. Through exposure to practical situations, the student teacher learns the complexities of teaching to the point where he can do a competent job of instruction.

7. Competent supervision must be provided if the student teacher is to attain the objectives of the student teaching course. This involves supervisory participation by the building principal, the classroom cooperating teacher and the college supervisor with free and open communication existing among all parties.

Terminology

The vocabulary of student teaching has not been completely standardized, although the terms used throughout this text are commonly accepted. In order to facilitate understanding and avoid misconceptions, the following definitions are those which will be followed in the ensuing pages.

Cooperating teacher--the classroom teacher in the public schools who is given the responsibility of working directly with the student teacher. Synonomous with this term is "supervising teacher" although some authorities reserve this title to teachers who work with student teachers in the campus laboratory school.

Professional laboratory experiences--all organized and directed activities of the prospective teacher which involve observation of, study about, and direct work with children and youth, leading to an increased understanding of the role of the teacher.

Observation--an experience in which the prospective teacher, with proper guidance and evaluation, increases his understanding of teaching by watching experienced teachers in their work. This is one of several professional laboratory experiences.

College supervisor--the designated faculty member of the teacher education institution who assumes the responsibility for supervising a number of student teachers. The college supervisor provides consultative assistance to both student teachers and cooperating teachers. Often this position is referred to as "university supervisor" or "campus supervisor."

Director of Student Teaching--the college or university administrative official who has the responsibility for screening of student teachers, coordinating the work of college supervisors, and making official contacts with representatives of the public schools.

Internship--a part of the professional education of teachers through an on-the-job experience in teaching for which the participant receives compensation for his work. The experience has appropriate supervision and guidance. Occasionally, student teachers are referred to as interns; however, this is not common usage since the student teacher receives no pay for his efforts.

ADDITIONAL REFERENCES

Andrews, Leonard O., *Student Teaching*, New York: The Center for Applied Research in Education, Inc., 1964.

Bennie, William A., "Student Teachers in Your Classrooms," *Overview*, 2:76-77, February, 1961.

Clarke, Charles M., Editor, *Teacher Education and the Public Schools*, 40th Yearbook, The Association for Student Teaching, 1961.

Flowers, John G., Chairman, *School and Community Laboratory Experiences in Teacher Education*, Report of the Sub-Committee of the Standards and Surveys Committee of the American Association of Teachers Colleges, Oneonta, New York, 1948.

Humphry, Betty J., "A Survey of Professional Education Offerings in NCATE-Accredited Institutions," *The Journal of Teacher Education*, 14:406-410, December, 1963.

Liggitt, William A., "An Evaluation of General Education in Elementary Teacher Preparation," *The Journal of Educational Research*, 57:156-159, November, 1963.

Malter, Morton S. and Troy L. Stearns, Editors, *Off-Campus Student Teaching*, 30th Yearbook, The Association for Student Teaching, 1951.

Rzepka, Louis, "The Campus School: Its Search for Identity," *The Journal of Teacher Education*, 13:24-29, March, 1962.

Schunk, Bernadene, Editor, *The Outlook in Student Teaching*, 41st Yearbook, The Association for Student Teaching, 1962, pp. 3-79.

Steeves, Frank L., *Issues in Student Teaching*, New York: The Odyssey Press, 1963.

Woodruff, Asahel D., *Student Teaching Today*, AACTE Study Series No. 5, Washington, D. C.: American Association of Colleges for Teacher Education, 1960.

Chapter II

The Roles of the Cooperating Agencies

Although the total student teaching experience is a cooperative venture, both the public schools and the teacher-preparation institutions have unique functions and responsibilities. In actual practice many of these are interrelated as they should be; however, unless responsibilities are clearly delineated and pointed up, confusion sometimes reigns and problems mount.

The public schools

Without the cooperation of the public schools, student teaching as it exists today could not be found. The role of the public schools as teacher educators is so much a part of the scene that teacher education would have to be radically altered if the public schools ceased to be a part of the picture.

The support which public schools have given to student teaching has been remarkable, so much so that the movement of student teaching from the campus to the public school classroom came about in an amazingly efficient operation, particularly so when one notes the lack of uniformity among colleges as to the amount of student teaching required, the time allotted for the experience, supervisory practices, and compensation provided for the cooperating teacher. While the public schools have accepted the challenge of teacher education willingly enough, they have often failed to analyze their responsibilities and facilities carefully enough to ascertain whether or not they should enter the picture of teacher education. This is not a role to be taken lightly, for the responsibility of providing the framework for the biggest course in professional education programs is indeed a sizable task.

Factors to be considered. When a public school agrees to accept student teachers, it also undertakes an implied obligation to provide adequate facilities for the program. This includes the development and maintenance of up-to-date school programs along with the teaching methods and materials which

reflect the most recent educational developments. It agrees to furnish high-quality supervision through its teaching faculty who have student teachers assigned to them. It also agrees to accept constructive suggestions from the college supervisors who work closely with the student teachers and the cooperating teachers, at least insofar as the work of the student teachers is concerned.

It should follow that the public school which agrees to these aspects of the student teaching program will have an improved educational program for its pupils, for most of these are the ingredients of a good educational program without the presence of student teachers as well as with them on the scene.

Another important consideration by the public schools in determining whether or not to cooperate in a student teaching program is not only a willingness to accept student teachers but a *desire* to help in this important undertaking. This desire must permeate the entire teaching staff, for the classroom teacher is the focal point of the student teaching experience. It is not enough for the school administration to voice an interest in cooperating in a student teaching program--such an interest must be echoed by the rank and file. Unless the teacher in the classroom is a willing and enthusiastic participant, the student teaching experience will not reach its potential.

Once this desire is present, the proper climate conducive to a successful student teaching experience is a foregone conclusion. The climate must be such that the student teacher feels welcome and wanted. Nothing can be more demoralizing to the student teacher nor affect his ultimate success more than a feeling of being imposed upon the cooperating teacher. No one feels comfortable when he feels he is intruding.

The question might be raised as to why the public schools should provide the facilities for student teaching. The most obvious answer is, of course, that the public schools have a vested interest in the quality and preparation of teachers who will be filling their classrooms in the future. Above and beyond this obvious answer is the issue of placing authority and responsibility for teacher education in general. Many authorities in student teaching point out that it has long been an accepted responsibility of the state to provide for teacher education. Since the public schools are state-created, state-controlled, and state-supported, what more logical provision could be made for student teaching than in the public schools?

From a practical standpoint, there are inherent advantages to the public schools in cooperating in a student teaching program. There is the opportunity for teachers to gain new insights and new ideas from their constant exposure to students fresh from the theory of the college classroom and from the college supervisors who work with them. An alert cooperating teacher can gain much in this way. If nothing else, the cooperating teachers usually take a long and intensive look at their own teaching since most of them take their new responsibility seriously and are eager to set a good example. This, too, often leads to an improved educational program since self-evaluation is an indispensible ingredient for self-improvement.

There are some educational administrators who like the youthful energy which student teachers bring into the classroom to say nothing of the recruitment value of being able to observe closely the teaching competency of prospective teachers soon to enter the classroom as fully-certificated teachers.

The decision to cooperate in a student teaching program usually requires a solution to the problem of what compensation, if any, should be given to the cooperating teachers for their added duties. A few schools reward such teachers with added increments on the salary schedule; however, these are not common practices. This does represent a possibility.

Many teacher-education institutions use various ways of providing compensation to the cooperating teachers; there is no common pattern. The 1951 Yearbook of The Association for Student Teaching listed twelve kinds of awards which various institutions have used in recognition of the services of the cooperating teacher. These were:

1. Paying money directly to the cooperating school or school district.
2. Awarding tuition credit to the cooperating teacher.
3. Awarding cash honorarium to the cooperating teacher.
4. Furnishing substitute teachers for the cooperating school.
5. Furnishing expense money for cooperating teachers' attendance at workshops, conferences, and conventions.
6. Housing public school students in college-owned buildings.
7. Granting to cooperating teachers the use of college facilities not offered to other teachers.

8. Supplying educational equipment, supplies, texts, and furniture.
9. Supplying occasional consultant services by college staff.
10. Awarding a four-year scholarship to a student of the cooperating school.
11. Awarding a cash honorarium to the cooperating principal.
12. Awarding credit toward the bachelor's degree to the cooperating teacher. [1]

Since this study was made there has been a noticeable trend toward eliminating any payment to cooperating teachers or to the school district. There is a growing list of teacher-education institutions who make no monetary remuneration or other compensation to the public school teachers who participate in the student teaching program. It is becoming increasingly recognized that this duty is a professional obligation of the classroom teacher and that the public schools have a professional duty to participate in the education of teachers. Philosophically, however, the exact role of the public schools in the education of teachers is still in a transitional stage.

One contributing factor to the elimination of cash honoraria is the fact that increasing enrollments in teacher education would create considerable budgetary problems if cooperating teachers were paid in cash, even though the amount paid in the past has been negligible. Many institutions have assessed a student teaching fee to the student teachers in order to obtain sufficient money to make even the small payment provided in the past. There is strong reluctance to increase such fees.

There is strong support for the principle of direct state subsidization of student teaching facilities in recognition of the state's responsibility in this area. Although this proposal has been debated since Haskew[2] first presented it, it has failed to make any impression in most states. It has led to a growing recognition of the state's role in the student teaching picture and a few states have taken steps toward assuming their share of the responsibility for student teaching. This may well be an indication of the shape of things to come.

[1] Morton S. Malter and Troy L. Stearns, Editors, Off-Campus Student Teaching, 30th Yearbook, The Association for Student Teaching, 1951, p. 58.

[2] Laurence D. Haskew, "Framework for Student Teaching: A Proposal," Education, November, 1949, pp. 150-154.

Even more recent is a proposal by Andrews[3] that federal aid be provided for subsidizing student teaching facilities, including the payment of some compensation to qualified cooperating teachers.

Another issue which confronts the public schools in the area of student teaching involves the legal status of the student teacher. Although every state has some requirement of student teaching for certification, very few have incorporated into existing legislation the legal provision for permitting student teachers, as unlicensed teachers, to teach in the public school classroom and have defined the rights and liabilities involved therein.

Although the student teaching requirement itself gives strong implication that such practice is permissable, specific reference to such practice has been found in only a few widely scattered states. This obvious paradox needs sorely to be explored and clarified by the various state legislatures or state boards of education. Litigation on the place of the student teacher in the classroom has been scarce and infrequent, indicating the general acceptance of the student teacher by all parties concerned. There are some authorities who express the opinion that the student teacher has the same rights, privileges, and liabilities as the certificated teacher if his place in the classroom has been approved by duly-authorized personnel of the public schools. So long as all parties concerned conduct the student teaching act in a reasonably prudent manner, liabilities are lessened. Administrators should emphasize to all teachers working with student teachers that they be particularly prudent about permitting student teachers to undertake teaching responsibilities involving dangerous exercises or experiments or the operation of dangerous equipment. If the cooperating teacher keeps a watchful eye on the activities of the student teacher and remains fully aware of all that is going on in the classroom, the legal status of the student teacher becomes more of an academic question than an actual problem.

Administrator responsibilities. Although much literature concerning student teaching discusses the role of the cooperating teacher, the place of the administrative officials of the schools is often overlooked. They, too, play important roles in the operation of a successful student teaching program.

[3] Leonard O. Andrews, "State and Federal Aid for Student Teaching--Now?" The Journal of Teacher Education, June, 1964, pp. 165-174.

The attitude of the school superintendent towards student teaching influences the attitudes of other administrators and teachers alike. He can do much to foster interest and enthusiasm toward the student teaching program. He can also, through his own efforts or through a designated representative, serve as a clearing house through which problems, suggestions, and communication in general may be channeled in both directions between colleges and the public schools.

A bulletin of the Association for Student Teaching lists several responsibilities of the superintendent of schools or his representative:

1. Interpreting the student teaching program to the community, board of education, and the teaching staff
2. Approving the selected corps of supervising teachers who will participate in the program
3. Participate in study groups to bring about changes and improvements in the program
4. Making available for study and distribution an excellent selection of printed materials which reflect current thinking on student teaching
5. Establishing rapport with the student teacher
6. Encouraging an exchange of ideas among all those concerned with student teaching so as to insure a program which can produce the caliber of teacher desired by any school system.[4]

It is particularly important that the superintendent pay attention to the first responsibility listed above. It is often necessary to explain the student teaching program to members of the board of education who are not as directly familiar with such programs as the superintendent. Their approval and support is essential. It is just as important that the community, particularly the parents, be made aware of the implications of student teaching in the schools. This can be done through P.T.A. meetings as well as in descriptive literature. Some parents might feel that the educational program will suffer with student teachers in charge of some of the instruction. Once they realize that the student teacher is given careful supervision and guidance and often teaches *with* the

[4] William S. Wagner, Vergil H. Hughes, and Gertrude B. Corcoran, Student Teaching: A Mission of the Elementary and Secondary Schools, Bulletin No. 13, The Association for Student Teaching, 1960, p. 5.

cooperating teacher, their fears are often overcome. No study has been found which indicated that pupil achievement suffered as a result of the participation of the classroom teacher in a student teaching situation.

Although not more important but certainly in a more strategic position to influence the student teaching experience directly is the building principal. Through his screening of prospective cooperating teachers, in-service education, and direct contacts with student teachers, the principal sets the tone for the program in his building. He should have frequent conferences with the college supervisor and should keep his finger on the pulse of the overall program in his building.

Much of the planned orientation of the student teacher, particularly in the school and school community, can best be provided by the building principal. Not only can he acquaint the student teacher with the personnel and program of the school, but he is also in a position to arrange observations with teachers who are involved in unique and outstanding classroom activities as well as to share his own professional experience in many ways.

Through both routine faculty meetings and special in-service education programs, he can develop insights and understandings on the part of his teaching staff concerning student teaching with a great influence on the actual work of the cooperating teacher with the prospective teacher assigned to him. Such meetings also provide avenues for the teaching faculty and the college supervisor to meet for mutual help and assistance.

Such meetings do not necessarily have to be restricted to those teachers who have student teachers during any given semester. Many other teachers are involved in the program through providing observation opportunities and in working with student teachers in extra-class activities. It is also one way of preparing such teachers for assuming the cooperating teacher's role at some future time.

Some principals take an active part in the actual teaching process in which the student teacher is involved. Through visitation and conferences they are able to exercise the same supervisory relationship which exists with regular faculty members. It should be pointed out, however, that the principal must not circumvent the cooperating teacher and should maintain open communication with both persons in the classroom as well as with the college supervisor.

One of the most important duties of the principal is to assist in the selection of the cooperating teacher. Although the final decision in this respect should be reached jointly by the college supervisor and the principal, the recommendation of the principal, who is thoroughly familiar with the abilities of the teaching staff, carries a great deal of weight. Because of this, it behooves the principal to recommend only those teachers who can do the job of supervision well. This means the careful screening of possibilities and the ultimate selection of only the best qualified. It is also implied that the principal must be kept informed as to the college expectations of the cooperating teacher and the qualities sought for this position. This approach obviously negates the practice of passing the cooperating position around among all teachers or assigning a student teacher to a weak teacher in hopes that the experience might strengthen him.

No teacher should be recommended for the supervisory job unless he has indicated a desire to work with a student teacher. In keeping with appropriate democratic procedures, the principal should confer with teachers who might serve as cooperating teachers and make certain of their cooperation in the student teaching endeavor. This does much to assure the proper human relationships which are important to the ultimate success of the college student.

Among the other important duties of the principal is the provision of time and opportunity to enable the cooperating teacher to do the job of supervision expected of him. Authorities recommend providing released time for this purpose as indicated in the Flowers report:

> The instructional load of all staff members. . . should be adjusted to provide for the including of activities with students in laboratory situations. Not only should the load of each staff member be adjusted to make it possible to include professional laboratory activities, but those activities should be considered a regular part of the teaching load.[5]

[5] John G. Flowers, Chairman, School and Community Laboratory Experiences in Teacher Education, Report of the sub-Committee of the Standards and Surveys Committee of the American Association of Teachers Colleges, 1948, pp. 332-333.

This is a costly and difficult thing to accomplish, however. Teachers can be released from other extra duties which will compensate to a slight extent for the added work of the student teaching supervision. It should be pointed out as well that there is some slight compensation in being relieved of some teaching and planning responsibilities when the student teacher has reached the point where he can assume some of these independently. This can be done without exploiting the student teacher and without offering any apologies.

There must be a meeting of the minds between the teacher education institution and the public schools in the administration of the student teaching program. The actual agreement may be reflected in a written contractual form or it may be an oral understanding. There is no preferred way of reaching decisions in this area; however, written agreements usually eliminate some confusion and more clearly delineate responsibilities and lines of communication. The form of the agreement is not so important as the operational relationships which evolve from the cooperative effort.

Regardless of the formality of the agreement, the rapport and genuine interest in teacher education on the part of both agencies must be such that the student teaching program will result in a high-level experience for the prospective teacher.

The college

The responsibilities of the college in the student teaching program are many. Among those which have been identified in one cooperative effort are the following, which call for the college to:

1. Screen carefully the ones who are to do student teaching. Those without ability or with personality defects and other disabilities that would make it impossible for them to become effective teachers should not be placed in the student teaching program.
2. Give sufficient preliminary education both in subject areas anu in professional areas so that student teachers will have a base to build upon.
3. Plan college work of student teachers so that sufficient time will be provided for them to carry out duties of student teaching...

4. Provide sufficient supervision for student teachers.
5. Cooperate with the. . . school administration in doing what may be necessary to ensure that the educational program contributes to the welfare of the school system and the effective learning of the pupils.
6. Provide educational leadership to all personnel in the teacher education program.[6]

High on the list of responsibilities of the college is the first one referred to above, screening carefully the ones who are to do student teaching. This has been a responsibility to which considerable lip-service has been devoted during the past several years with little actually being done to carry out the responsibility with all of its implications. Grade-point averages in college work has been the primary screening implement with some colleges requiring physical examinations and speech tests. During the past few years, however, colleges are becoming increasingly aware that such perfunctory screening is not sufficient to insure highly-qualified professional teachers. Those who work with student teachers have been aware for some time that personality aspects of the potential teacher are nearly as significant as the knowledge he possesses, and a serious effort is being made to make the screening process broader and more intensive at the same time. As a part of this screening process, prospective teachers are sometimes identified early in their college careers and some screening takes place long before the time of student teaching has arrived.

No one seems to know the best way of screening prospective teachers. Many institutions use admission boards who interview and approve candidates for teacher certification. Sometimes included in the assessment data are various personality and aptitude tests which give an indication of the student's potential.

Once student teachers have been selected, the college has the responsibility of assigning them to situations where they have the opportunity of seeing quality teaching, well-qualified teachers, and have an open field for their own personal development into competent classroom instructors. This is not an easy task, for the identification of competent cooperating

[6] Procedures for the Implementation of Professional Laboratory Experiences, Mimeographed, Austin Independent School District, Austin, Texas, 1962, pp. 5-6.

teachers who desire to work with student teachers is reported regularly as a significant and serious problem confronting the administrators of student teaching programs as indicated earlier.

This calls for the college supervisor to take advantage of the building principal's knowledge of his teachers as the two cooperate in placement. Unfortunately, even with the best of information, there are sometimes errors in judgment in the placement of student teachers. Personal compatibility is essential to success in student teaching, yet no one can predict how two personalities will interact. When conflicts occur, they should be recognized as early as possible and changes made in the assignment if they appear necessary.

Such personality clashes do not necessarily reflect incompetency on the part of either cooperating teacher or student teacher. As a general rule, however, it is thought that student teachers should make a determined effort to adjust to any situation since the teaching role in itself involves such adjustment to many personalities of pupils, parents, other teachers, and administrative personnel. This again reflects the need for adequate communication among all parties.

The college supervisor's responsibility does not end with the assignment of the student teacher to the public school classroom; it also includes careful and frequent supervision. Both the student teacher and the classroom teacher need assistance from the college if the experience is to reach maximum expectations. The student teacher-supervisor ratio must be reasonable enough to permit regular contacts. The recognition of this adds to the cost of the student teaching program, a factor which has resulted in many institutions' maintaining supervisory loads which are untenable if proper supervision is to be provided. Many authorities agree that supervisory efficiency is impaired proportionately for every student teacher over twenty in a full supervisory load for the college supervisor.

When supervisory loads are too heavy, it is to be expected that the supervisor will take unwise short-cuts in his supervision. The most common result of a large supervisory load is the lack of frequent visits to observe the student teacher in action. Such visits are necessary for evaluating student teacher progress, keeping acquainted with the activities in the classroom, and providing for conferences with both the student teacher and the cooperating teacher. If the college supervisor spends two hours per week with each student teacher, including time spent in classroom visitation and conferences, it may easily be seen that it would require a 40-hour week to work with 20 student teachers. This does not allow time for travel between schools, for consultative work with teachers, for conducting seminars, nor for other duties in committees normally expected of college faculty members, to say nothing of productive work which individuals may be expected to do. One can see that the conscientious supervisor is a busy person indeed.

Because of all they try to accomplish, some supervisors tend to neglect those student teachers who are with superior cooperating teachers and spend more time with those who are having problems or with teachers who desire more help and assistance in working with student teachers. One might question the wisdom of such a practice since it is the same philosophy a teacher might adopt by working only with remedial pupils in his class while neglecting the more gifted. Each student teacher needs his share of supervisory help from both the college supervisor and the cooperating teacher.

If campus supervision is to be effective and helpful, those who are assigned to this responsibility must be sufficiently competent to be of help to those in the classroom. This would suggest that teacher-education institutions recognize the supervisory role as an important one and utilize their best staff members for this function. One might question an excessive number of graduate students performing this task which is the practice in many large institutions. The prestige of the college supervisor as well as the quality of his work is dependent upon experience and preparation for the job just as is any other professional assignment. The concept of supervision as an occasional visit or as "dropping by" has no place in a high quality student teaching program.

There are a few instances where public schools and colleges have employed supervisors cooperatively to supervise the student teaching experience. Such a practice has much in its favor since it provides the supervisor with an official relationship to the classroom teacher; however, there are attendant dangers which must be recognized and avoided. Such a practice might develop into a supervisor-teacher relationship which loses much of the rapport that often exists when the supervisor is not in an administratively superior position. Supervisory loads must be such that the supervisor can do a reasonable job in his work rather than commensurate with those which public school supervisors often have. In other words, a jointly-employed supervisor must clearly be a *student teaching supervisor* and be allowed to perform this function.

Colleges must be certain that all parties concerned have full orientation as to what is expected of them. Student teachers need to be prepared for their assignments and informed of correct procedures, professional ethics, and the boundaries within which they must perform their teaching duties. Cooperating teachers must be acquainted with the program, with their responsibilities, and must know what the college expects of them with respect to the planning, observation, and the actual teaching of the student teacher.

The publication of a cooperating teacher's handbook, which is common practice, will aid in giving these teachers an idea of their role in the student teaching picture; but the most important contribution in this area must come from the college supervisor who has the opportunity of working closely with the classroom teacher in implementing all aspects of the program. Cooperating teachers have frequently listed the lack of orientation to their roles as a persistent problem.

The college has an obligation to provide some formal preparation for the cooperating teacher. Many institutions offer specific courses in the supervision of student teaching--a practice which has been quite successful. These may be offered during summer sessions or at night or late afternoon during the academic year. To expect cooperating teachers to do a quality job and not provide opportunities for them to become qualified to do it is an incongruous position. An obvious problem is getting cooperating teachers to attend such courses or workshops. Since the college has no direct authority over the teachers, it must depend upon their interest and professional involvement to secure participation. If the college gives worthwhile instruction, however, the course will sell itself.

Another obligation which colleges must assume is the development of a student teaching program of such a nature that the objectives of the course may be reached. Specifically, this means organizing student teaching in such a way that prospective teachers have the opportunity of doing the many things expected of them. Many colleges, for example, lament the fact that cooperating teachers do not have enough conferences with student teachers while at the same time they maintain a program which requires the student teacher to be on the job only a fraction of the school day while taking other college courses. Such a program also limits the experiences of the student teacher in becoming familiar with the total role of the teacher, in observing other teachers, in participating in the extra-curricular program, and in taking part in faculty meetings, all of which are often stated as expectations of the student teaching role.

The college best operates the student teaching program if its own administrative channels are clearly delineated. Usually the program is more successful if there is one central office through which all matters pertaining to student teaching are channeled with one person designated to coordinate the program. This person is usually known as a Coordinator or Director of Student Teaching. This centralization of responsibility avoids duplication of effort and simplifies communication to and from the public schools. A decentralized student teaching organization usually creates additional annoyances and problems in working with the public schools.

It behooves the teacher preparation institution to keep in mind that its relationship with the public schools, while cooperative insofar as the student teaching experience is concerned, is a guest status with respect to the school and its curriculum. The college cannot cooperate with a school in student teaching while at the same time be openly critical about the school and its program. If such criticism is justified, the college should not place student teachers in such a program. On the other hand, if the public school desires to make improvements in its program and invites the college to participate through the student teaching supervisory program in improving the educational program, the college should make any suggestions or contribution which it can.

Provision should be made by the teacher education institution for the public schools to have a voice in determining the policies affecting the operation of the student teaching program. Not only does this reflect the best of democratic procedures, but it also has the practical effect of keeping communication channels open and assures the college that proposed changes will be accepted by those who work directly with student teachers. This is the only way, also, for providing the continuous evaluation of the overall program which is desirable.

Joint responsibilities

It should be obvious from what has been said that both the public schools and the teacher-education institutions must work closely in the operation of a successful student teaching program. Most of the responsibilities are joint even though each has its own peculiar areas in which it must take the initiative. The following chart indicates the responsible role of each agency in the student teaching program. It may be seen that many areas require the two parties to work closely together, each contributing its own efforts toward a cooperative, productive program.

DESIGNATED RESPONSIBILITIES OF THE STUDENT TEACHING PROGRAM

	Responsibility	Public School	College
1.	Selection of student teaching center		X
2.	Selection of student teachers		X
3.	Selection of cooperating teacher	X	
4.	Assignment of student teacher		X
5.	Planning the overall program	X	X
6.	Providing in-service education for teachers	X	X
7.	Arranging observations	X	
8.	Directing daily work of student teacher	X	
9.	Planning with the student teacher	X	X
10.	Conducting accompanying seminar		X
11.	Evaluation of student teaching	X	X
12.	Providing professional consultation		X
13.	Interpreting program to the community	X	

It is not intended that the above chart designate sole responsibilities of each agency but rather that it indicate those in which initiative should be taken by each party in the student teaching program. A full realization of the need for cooperative effort by both agencies involved will do much to improve the quality of the teachers who will fill the classrooms of the future.

ADDITIONAL REFERENCES

Andrews, Leonard O., "State and Federal Aid for Student Teaching--Now?" *The Journal of Teacher Education*, 15:165-174, June, 1964.

Batchelder, Howard T., Richard E. Lawrence, and George R. Myers, *A Guide to Planning for Off-Campus Student Teaching*, Bulletin No. 11, The Association for Student Teaching, 1959.

Bennie, William A., "Teacher Education and the Student Teaching Program," *The American School Board Journal*, 144:18, April, 1962.

Brown, William B., Mildred Naslund, and Nellie Dederick, "Los Angeles City Schools--Partner in Teacher Education," *The Journal of Teacher Education*, 12:60-65, March, 1961.

Clarke, Charles M., Editor, *Teacher Education and the Public Schools*, 40th Yearbook, The Association for Student Teaching, 1961, pp. 97-114; 141-163.

Curtis, Dwight K., Editor, *Achieving Quality in Off-Campus Professional Laboratory Experiences*, Bulletin No. 8, The Association for Student Teaching, 1957.

DelPopolo, Joseph A. and Maurie Wilson, "Student Teaching and the Role of The Public Schools," *New York State Education*, 51:14-16, March, 1964.

Grayson, William H. Jr., "Student Teaching--Increasing Responsibility," *High Points*, 44:28-32, June, 1962.

Haskew, Laurence D., "Framework for Student Teaching: A Proposal," *Education*, 70:150-154, November, 1949.

Schunk, Bernadene, Editor, *The Outlook in Student Teaching*, 41st Yearbook, The Association for Student Teaching, 1962, pp. 131-155.

Schwartz, Sheila, "The Principal's Role in the Student Teaching Program," *The Journal of Teacher Education*, 13:78-81, March, 1962.

Wagner, William, Vergil H. Hughes, and Gertrude B. Corcoran, *Student Teaching: A Mission of the Elementary and Secondary Schools*, Bulletin No. 13, The Association for Student Teaching, 1960.

Chapter III

The Cooperating Teacher

The focal point of a successful student teaching experience is the cooperating teacher in whose classroom the student teacher is assigned. This responsibility is indeed great, for the freedom and guidance given by the one who sees the student teacher daily can open the door to a high degree of enthusiasm about teaching with resultant success. Working with a student teacher offers the classroom teacher the opportunity of making significant contributions to teaching as well as offering an exciting experience in broadening his own horizons.

Many teachers look forward to the chance of working with a prospective teacher for the mere pleasure of association with the college student. It offers a delightful change of pace from the daily teaching responsibilities and presents a different teaching challenge. In the final analysis, however, it is another opportunity to teach.

Various lists of criteria may be found for the selection of the cooperating teacher. Most colleges insist that the cooperating teacher have a minimum amount of teaching experience--usually at least three years. Possession of a master's degree is also desirable; however, most colleges accept teachers who lack the advanced degree. The bachelor's degree should be required of all cooperating teachers and usually is the minimal acceptable educational level. Colleges seek cooperating teachers who have shown evidence of genuine professional interest and have positive attitudes toward teaching and toward working with student teachers. It is essential that a teacher supervising student teachers be able to demonstrate the elements of good teaching and the ability to analyze basic principles of teaching and learning. The teacher selected should be willing to give the necessary time and energy in working with the student teacher to insure a maximum learning opportunity.

The cooperating teacher may be motivated to accept a student teacher by any one of several reasons. He may feel pressure from his administrative superior to do the job; he may desire the small compensation which the college pays; he may want someone to do some of his work for him; he may feel a professional obligation to work with student teachers or he may enjoy the role of cooperating teacher. It is to be hoped that the latter two reasons are the motivational forces behind his actions, but a frank appraisal must include the other reasons as occasional factors for some teachers' acceptance of student teachers. The college is understandably wary about putting student teachers with those teachers whose motivation is suspect and less than professional.

Whatever his motivation, there are rewards to the cooperating teacher. Among the opportunities for professional and personal growth which accrue from the supervision of student teachers are the following which were identified by a group of cooperating teachers in a recent study:

Personal and/or Professional Benefit[1]

Personal and/or Professional Benefit	Frequency
1. Keep up with current trends	41
2. Work to capacity and evaluate own teaching	35
3. Improve academic background	33
4. Resource person for professional education classes	24
5. Carry on experimentation in classroom	24
6. Resource person for professional meetings	23
7. Learn to adjust to individuals	15
8. More time to work with individual children in the class	11
9. Working on college committees	9

All who work with student teaching realize the importance and value of the cooperating teacher. Indeed, there have been studies which indicate that the cooperating teacher is the most influential factor in determining the kind of teaching done by the student teacher once he assumes a teaching position of his own. This includes his attitude toward teaching and toward children as well. It is obvious, therefore, that working with a student teacher is an important challenge.

[1] Ernest J. Milner, Editor, The Supervising Teacher, 38th Yearbook, The Association for Student Teaching, 1959, p. 21.

The cooperating teacher has three loyalties which he must honor. His first obligation is to the pupils in his classes whom he is employed to teach; his second is to himself and the maintenance of his professional reputation and integrity; the third loyalty is to his student teacher and to the improvement of his chosen profession. In a properly oriented student teaching experience there need be no division of loyalty on the part of the cooperating teacher. Both the cooperating teacher and the student teacher should be equally concerned about the teaching-learning situation, and their joint efforts should lead to the improvement of learning. If the cooperating teacher participates with the student teaching program as he should, the overall guidance of the classroom progress will still be very much under his control. All of this contributes to the growth of the student teacher and the continued professionalization of the classroom teacher. Actually, the student teacher may make significant contributions to the activities of the class thus enhancing the learning opportunities offered the pupils.

The cooperating teacher should be one who possesses commendable teaching skill. In addition, he must understand teacher education and know something about the purposes and procedures of the student teaching experience. These, coupled with a willingness to share his knowledge and skills with the student teacher, should make for a pleasant teaching experience for both parties.

The cooperating teacher has the final authority over what occurs in his classroom, with the possible exception of the building principal. If the relationship which exists between the cooperating teacher and other parties of the student teaching program are what they should be, this should cause no problem. It remains, however, that the cooperating teacher has been legally employed and is paid for teaching his classes. His is the legal and moral responsibility for seeing that the children in his care have competent teaching. If this becomes a matter of judgment, his judgment prevails.

This points up the necessity for good human relations in the student teaching situation. The importance of this was reported by Dickson in a study made at Stanford University. After interviewing a number of student teachers, cooperating teachers, and college supervisors, he reported several conclusions concerning human relations. Among them were:

1. Human relations difficulties were a major characteristic of the student teaching program.... Two out of three interview responses of those participating in this study referred to instances of dissatisfaction in their relationship to others.
2. Problems of individual adjustment, program or work dissatisfaction, and communication were the three general problem areas revealed in the comments of student teachers, supervising teachers, and supervisors...

. . . .

3. The distinct principal problems which appear in the human relations of student-teachers, supervising teachers, and supervisors with others are not similar, generally, in every relationship.
   A. Student teachers--(1) Want specific help with problems and sympathetic understanding from supervisors. (2) Desire to please supervising teachers and wish to establish pleasant relations with them.
   B. Supervising teachers--(1) Are interested mainly in the preparation and achievement of student teachers in practice-teaching. (2) Are insecure in their relations with supervisors. (3) Want supervisors to ease their insecurity by offering suggestions and solving problems.
   C. Supervisors--(1) Desire to see student teachers achieve successful teaching methods. (2) Are mainly concerned over the insecurity of supervising teachers and express hostility and disagreement in discussing them.

   . . . .

4. Some student-teachers experience difficulty because they do not realistically face the fact that they are beginners in teaching and feel that they are expected to emulate or teach as expertly as the supervising teacher....
5. On the contrary, other student teachers have the tendency to adopt attitudes of superiority in comparing their work with that of supervising teachers. No other single attitude will as quickly develop hostility, disagreement, and conflict in the student teaching situation.

6. Student teachers do not adapt readily to the differences in educational philosophy and methodology which are found in the public school classrooms. Consequently, they experience hostility, disagreement, and conflict in the student teaching situation.[2]

It was evident in this study that all parties desired for the student teacher to succeed but felt insecure in their respective relationships in promoting that success. It was also obvious that the need for improved understanding and communication contributed to this insecurity. It is suggested that the findings of this study are applicable to many student teaching situations and that careful study of the conclusions might have interesting implications for college supervisors and cooperating teachers.

It is hoped that the cooperating teacher feels free to call upon the college supervisor for assistance not only in determining the student teaching program but also in improving the learning situation. In the final analysis, the cooperating teacher has the responsibility for the instruction of the class; the college supervisor has the responsibility for the student teacher and his preparation. Since the two are so closely interrelated, the necessity of good communication and mutual understanding is great.

In understanding the purposes of student teaching and the emphases in supervision, the cooperating teacher should realize that his supervision lies in the development of broad understandings of the basic principles underlying the teaching-learning situation rather than providing the student teacher with a bag of tricks or specific prescriptions for everything which might occur in the classroom. This point of view is described in the 38th Yearbook of the Association for Student Teaching which lists the principles of supervision of student teaching as:

1. The aim of student teaching supervision is to enable the prospective teacher to become skilled in the improvement of the teaching-learning process and the total setting for learning.
2. The present program of supervised teaching focuses on the teaching-learning situation rather than on the

[2] George E. Dickson, "The Crux of an Effective Off-Campus Student Teaching Program," Educational Administration and Supervision, March, 1953, pp. 141-143.

individual. The supervising and student teacher are co-workers aiming at the improvement of the learning situation.

3. The modern supervisor of student teaching directs the beginning teacher's attention toward the fundamentals of education and orients the student teacher to the nature of learning and its improvement within the general aims of education.
4. Current emphasis is on the student teacher assuming his rightful place as a cooperating member of the school which is concerned with the improvement of teaching through greater knowledge of the teaching-learning process.[3]

This does not mean that the student teacher does not learn specific approaches to teaching nor even some techniques and "gimmicks"; however, these are based on sound principles of learning so that the student teacher knows why they work and how they may be adapted to other situations. Such techniques are secondary to the primary objectives of the experience.

The role of the cooperating teacher is summarized in a bulletin of the Association for Student Teaching. It includes:

1. Planning for the initial orientation of the student teacher to the classroom and to the school
2. Acquainting himself with the program of student teaching as proposed by the college
3. Familiarizing himself with the background of the student teacher (through materials sent by the college)
4. Creating an atmosphere of acceptance of the student on the part of himself, the pupils, the faculty and the community
5. Introducing the student teacher to classroom routines and instructional procedures
6. Providing opportunities for observation and participation on the part of the student teacher in various classes and extra-class activities
7. Acquainting the student teacher with pupil personnel records and the manner in which they are kept and used
8. Acquainting the student teacher with instructional materials, supplies and equipment available to him

[3] Milner, op. cit., p. 25.

10. Establishing a climate in which the student teacher may gradually develop skill in planning and continuously evaluate his own planning procedures
11. Treating the student teacher as a co-worker rather than as a subordinate
12. Providing opportunities for the student teacher to test theory in practice in a variety of classroom and extra-class situations
13. Arranging the schedule for actual teaching experiences by the student teacher
14. Providing for continuous evaluation of the student's teaching through frequent, planned conferences, weekly report sheets, self-evaluation by the student teacher, and check lists
15. Guiding the student teacher in attaining cooperatively established objectives
16. Providing opportunities for professional growth through attendance at professional meetings, staff meetings, use of the library, and by building a personal library
17. Providing opportunities and time for conferences with the student teacher
18. Serving as consultant to former students in in-service situations.[4]

It is difficult to measure the amount of assistance and help which the cooperating teacher actually provides to the student teacher. In one study, based on the judgments of 171 student teachers, the following areas were identified in which the co-operating teachers provide assistance. These are listed in rank order with the areas of most help listed first:[5]

1. Adjusting to the teaching role
2. Selection of content to be taught
3. Understanding boys and girls
4. Selecting teaching materials
5. Evaluating my own teaching
6. Selecting teaching procedures (methods)
7. Motivating pupil interest and response
8. Determining the objectives of lessons

[4] Dwight K. Curtis, Editor, Achieving Quality in Off-Campus Professional Laboratory Experiences, Bulletin No. 8, Association for Student Teaching, 1957, pp. 23-24.

[5] William A. Bennie, An Analysis of Student Teaching and Supervision at The University of Texas, Multilithed, The University of Texas, 1964, pp. 31-32.

9. Making daily lesson plans
10. Determining pupil grades
11. Planning long range instruction
12. Understanding the purposes of education
13. Constructing tests and examinations

This same study indicated that the college supervisor provided more help in some of these areas which were concerned with broader aspects of the teaching role such as understanding the purposes of education, planning long range instruction, and determining the objectives of lessons.

Both supervisors need to cooperate in providing help in these and other areas. The cooperating teacher should keep in mind that the college supervisor is interested only in the student teacher and his effectiveness and growth. He has usually seen hundreds of teachers in his work and deals with each one individually in his own situation. The fact that the cooperating teacher has been selected for work with a student teacher should reassure him that the supervisor has confidence in him and that he is thought competent to do the job.

If proper communication exists, there should be no conflict or insecurity felt. Both parties are interested in the achievement of the pupils and the success of the student teacher. This is a real team effort insofar as the development of the prospective teacher is concerned.

Cooperating teachers should find out from the college supervisor the procedures desired with respect to the kinds of experiences planned for the student teacher, the planning involved, conferences to be held, etc. Tentative plans for the student teacher's development should be cooperatively blocked out for the entire period of student teaching as early as possible. The amount of responsibility in the actual supervision of classroom work by each party should be determined as well. Once these guidelines are formulated, the relationship should run smoothly with each supervisor fully aware of his own responsibilities.

ADDITIONAL REFERENCES

Curtis, Dwight K. and Leonard O. Andrews, *Guiding Your Student Teacher,* New York: Prentice-Hall, Inc., 1954.

Dickson, George E., "The Crux of an Effective Off-Campus Student Teaching Program," *Educational Administration and Supervision*, 39:139-146, March, 1953.

Haines, Aleyne, *Guiding the Student Teaching Process in Elementary Education*, Chicago: Rand McNally Publishing Co., 1960.

Lamb, Pose, *The Student Teaching Process in Elementary Schools*, Columbus, Ohio: Charles E. Merrill Books, Inc., 1965.

Milner, Ernest J., Editor, *The Supervising Teaching,* 38th Yearbook, Association for Student Teaching, 1959.

Myers, George R. and William J. Walsh, *Student Teaching and Internship in Today's Secondary Schools*, Columbus, Ohio: Charles E. Merrill Books, Inc., 1964.

Price, Robert D., "The Influence of Supervising Teachers," *The Journal of Teacher Education*, 12:471-475, December, 1961.

Taylor, Gem Kate, "Factors in the Decision to Become a Supervising Teacher," *Peabody Journal of Education*, 38:351-352, May, 1961.

Chapter IV

The College Supervisor

Unless they are conducted under the careful supervision of persons who have insights into the facets of good teaching, the experiences of student teaching lose much of their significance. Otherwise bad habits of teaching, poor procedures, and naive expectations of pupil progress may be developed and perpetuated. This is the principal reason why colleges are reluctant to grant on-the-job credit in student teaching to persons teaching on emergency or temporary certificates. Student teaching is much more than trial-and-error experimentation - hence, the inclusion of the two supervisory positions, the cooperating teacher and the college supervisor.

It is sometimes difficult to differentiate between the functions of the two supervisory roles. Indeed, their responsibilities and functions vary from institution to institution; however, there appears to be general acceptance of the need for both and some common agreement as to what part each plays in the overall student teaching experience.

The supervisory job

As the college representative, the college supervisor carries the responsibility of the overall supervisory instruction provided the student teacher. This includes taking the preliminary steps of assignment, selection, and orientation as well as close surveillance of the development of the student teacher's learning experiences and the concurrent evaluation of his progress.

Desirable practices. It is the responsibility of the college supervisor to see that student teachers under his supervision are prepared for their student teaching experience. This involves a planned orientation. Such orientation should include not only an understanding of the expectations of student teaching but also familiarization with the total role of the teacher.

Pertinent to this area is an awareness of dress and grooming, professional ethics, relationships with pupils and staff members, as well as acquaintance with rules and regulations peculiar to student teachers in specific schools.

Student teachers should have an understanding of the objectives of student teaching and be acquainted with the type of activities which help attain these objectives. They should know the general procedure involved in working with the supervisor and the classroom cooperating teacher with respect to developing plans, having conferences, and the transitional steps involved in working towards acquiring major teaching responsibilities.

It is also helpful if student teachers are acquainted with the evaluation form used in evaluating their efforts. This will promote the utilization of the evaluation form as a means of self-evaluation throughout the student teaching period.

Some supervisors from the college require student teachers to maintain daily logs or diaries in which a careful record of the student teaching experience is outlined. Such a practice enables the supervisor to keep up-to-date with the student teacher's varied activities and helps the student teacher evaluate his past activities. Some supervisors require students to keep notebooks or files of plans, materials, and evaluations of the various aspects of their teaching. Such practices as these can be helpful to both supervisor and student teacher if they are used properly. Care must be taken to see that such requirements serve a useful purpose and do not constitute busywork.

It is suggested that the college supervisor keep a file on each of his student teachers with a record of visitation observations and of conferences with the student. Such detailed information is not only useful in planning with the prospective teacher for future growth but is also helpful in evaluating the student teaching experience.

The Association for Student Teaching reported a survey of one hundred thirty cooperating teachers concerning their reactions to the responsibilities of the college supervisor. They reported that they felt the college supervisor should:

1. Visit the classroom of the supervising teacher frequently enough to become acquainted with the students and their teaching practices.
2. Provide the supervising teacher with pertinent information about the student teacher.

3. Share responsibility of evaluation of the student teacher with the principal, the supervising teacher, and the student teacher.
4. Help the supervising teacher understand and play her role in the student teaching program.
5. Help the supervising teacher and the student teacher resolve any problems which develop in the student teaching experience.
6. Acquaint the supervising teacher with what is expected from the student teacher--diaries, evaluations, reports, and the like.
7. Be willing and able to make suggestions for the improvement of instruction in the classroom of the supervising teacher.
8. Help the supervising teacher and the principal provide opportunities for the student teacher to participate in varied and extensive activities in the total school program.
9. Provide sources of information as requested by the supervising teacher or the student teacher.
10. Observe the prospective supervising teacher in action several times prior to any student teaching assignment.
11. Place the student teacher with the supervising teacher who can provide high quality teaching experiences.
12. Help the principal in his preparation for the induction of the student teacher into his school program.
13. Consult and advise with the student teacher as the occasion dictates.
14. Observe the student teacher in action and follow the observations with a three-or-four-way conference.
15. Help the college understand and discharge its responsibilities to the student teaching program in the laboratory and cooperating schools.[1]

Human relationships. The college supervisor treads a precarious path. He has the responsibility for seeing that the student teacher secures the kind of experience which will prepare him for successful teaching, yet he has no direct authority over the classroom situation in which the student is working in most cases. In reaching the expectations of his job, he

[1] Ernest J. Milner, Editor, The Supervising Teacher, 38th Yearbook, The Association for Student Teaching, 1959, p. 91.

must utilize all the tact, diplomacy, and understanding possible. As an "ambassador without portfolio" he has a demanding position.

The classroom teacher's suspicion of supervision in general which has been bred from authoritarian practices in the past, coupled with the insecurity of working under the eye of an "expert" from the college campus, must be overcome quickly and pleasantly if the relationship between the cooperating teacher and the college supervisor is to produce the desired results. The college supervisor must always remember that the classroom is the teacher's kingdom and that any suggestions for change in procedure must be carefully made. The focal point for all such discussions should be the student teacher's experience rather than the teacher's approach. It is not the function of the college supervisor to perform voluntary missionary service to the public schools. If he is asked for suggestions, he should feel free to make them; but his major responsibility is to secure the best possible experience for the student teacher while maintaining the best possible public relations between the public school and the college.

The study by Dickson referred to earlier included some conclusions pertinent to this area for college supervisors. These were:

1. Communication dissatisfaction on the part of the student-teachers and supervisors appears to be a situation of mutual misunderstanding of the initiatory role in providing adequate opportunities for student-supervisor contacts....
2. The emotional needs of security, recognition, and understanding in student teachers are not recognized or successfully met by supervisors who are mainly interested in student teaching ability.

. . . .

3. The inability of the supervisor to recognize the close alignment which exists between a student-teacher and a supervising teacher is a major cause of possible hostility toward the supervisor and the rejection of his ideas on the part of the student or supervising teacher.

. . . .

4. In many cases, much of the hostility, insecurity, and anxiety which supervising teachers display are the result of ineffective lines of communication between supervising teachers and supervisors.

5. Supervising teachers and supervisors are mutually anxious to feel wanted and secure with each other in the student-teaching program. Failures on the part of supervisors to give supervising teachers direction or to provide assurance of work well done are the primary factors restricting the establishment of good relations..[2]

The college supervisor can promote good human relations by including all parties in the student teaching team in the planning and evaluative aspects of the experience. Three-way conferences in which each participant is encouraged to contribute his suggestions do much to keep the air cleared and to avoid misunderstandings. He must keep in mind that the supervising teacher has much at stake and also has ideas, convictions, and perhaps as many biases as does the college supervisor. These must be considered.

Good supervision is based on mutual respect, cooperative efforts, and a common understanding of the goals, the approaches to those goals, and the progress being made toward their attainment.

The student teaching seminar. Most student teaching programs include regular seminar or discussion meetings between the college supervisor and the student teachers in his care. If these are well-planned, they do much to relate practice to theory and to increase the student teachers' understanding of what they are asked to do. Such seminars also offer excellent opportunities for evaluating observations and answering questions arising from them.

As much as possible, seminar discussions should evolve around common problems of teaching rather than individual problems. The latter should be discussed in conference with those primarily concerned. The common problems which arise from the teaching experience of the group provide ample material for worthwhile discussion, although skill is necessary in identifying them and in guiding the discussion toward proper conclusions.

Most student teachers need help during seminar discussions with such problems as planning their work, selecting materials, adapting the work to the level and understanding of their pupils,

[2] George E. Dickson, "The Crux of an Effective Off-Campus Student Teaching Program," Educational Administration and Supervision, March, 1953, pp. 143-144.

and evaluating pupil progress. Much can be done to relate basic principles of teaching and learning previously studied in professional courses to actual practice in the classroom. The seminar should synthesize the students' professional study into a workable and effective teaching performance.

There are other areas which may be incorporated into class discussion which are illustrative of the student teachers' concerns. Usually the problem of pupil behavior is raised and "discipline" needs to be discussed and related to their study of child behavior. Student teachers also become very interested in securing teaching positions, and, unless provision is made elsewhere to acquaint them with the procedures involved, some time may be profitably spent in this area. A step can be made toward the professionalization of the teacher by acquainting him with the ethical aspects of teaching.

Care should be taken in seminar discussions to avoid discussion of specific personalities and schools. Proper ethical consideration requires that discussion be impersonal and professional. Cooperating teachers are sometimes sensitive about the seminar classes unless they are fully acquainted with the nature and the purposes of the discussion groups.

Many supervisors include the cooperating teachers in the seminars on occasion and invite individual teachers to participate in the class as consultants in areas of their special interests or talents. Such practice is desirable. Indeed there are isolated instances where institutions have met with cooperating teachers in seminar rather than with student teachers which adds an entirely new perspective to the seminar role. Such a practice as this has many interesting possibilities.

The seminar also provides an excellent opportunity for student teachers to share ideas, materials, and observations about lessons and teaching in general. Many are teaching in similar situations and are eager to find out what other student teachers are doing in related classes. The supervisor must keep in mind that student teachers can learn from one another.

Patterns of supervision

Prevailing practice reflects two differing patterns of campus supervision. One pattern employs educational specialists in the various subject areas as college supervisors while the second pattern utilizes general supervisory personnel where college supervisors cut across subject matter lines. Each pattern has distinct implications for the kind of supervisory approach and the kind of supervisory personnel needed.

Although practices vary, some criteria for the selection of the college supervisor may be identified. In high priority is the personality of the supervisor, for his ability to relate with others undergirds his effectiveness in other aspects. He should also have a good knowledge of the latest developments in learning theory backed up by several years of actual classroom teaching experience. As a member of the college faculty he should have a minimum of the master's degree with the doctorate desirable. His status as an educator must be such that he can command the respect of the classroom teachers with whom he will be working. He should also have experience in working with student teachers, both as a cooperating teacher and as a college supervisor if possible. It is in the area of academic specialization that the criteria for general and special supervisors differ.

General college supervision. The pattern of general college supervision is probably the more common one. This is probably true, however, for economic reasons rather than educational reasons, although some authorities believe that this pattern avoids possible conflict between the two supervisory positions somewhat better than specialized supervision. As off-campus student teaching programs have grown in size and number, general supervision has been found to predominate. Since several student teachers, teaching in various subject fields, are often assigned to a specific off-campus center, the economics of sending one supervisor to work with the total group rather than several different supervisors in specialized areas is obvious. Not only is money saved in travel expenses but valuable time of college faculty is conserved.

This same philosophy often results in the general supervisor having a somewhat larger supervisory load than is found in other patterns. If the number of student teachers assigned to a specific center is two or three over the usual supervisory load, the one supervisor usually assumes this as a part of his assignment rather than having a second supervisor go off-campus to accommodate the two or three additional student teachers. It would appear that, by the same token, occasionally loads are under the acceptable size thus reducing the supervisory load. In practice, however, this seldom seems to happen since colleges are reluctant to permit faculty members to have less than a full load of teaching or supervisory responsibilities.

The question of the desirability of general supervision over specialized supervision was raised by Pfeiffer who asked:

> If the college supervisor is to supplement the contributions of the supervising teacher, should not his abilities be in different areas? Might conflicts be avoided if the supervising teacher were described as being a subject matter specialist and the college supervisor described as a specialist in the teaching-learning process and in teaching others to teach?[3]

This points up the concept of supervision usually held when general supervisory patterns prevail. The college supervisor is considered an authority in Education and in student teaching as an aspect of teacher education. His responsibility insofar as the classroom itself is concerned evolves around the overall guidance of the student teaching experience including taking the initiative in planning the types of experiences in which the student teacher should participate, evaluating those experiences and in making suggestions concerning the teaching-learning situation as it is reflected through the student teacher's work. Since he is often supervising in subject areas outside his field of academic competency, he is not expected to assume the role of academic expert and leaves this function to the cooperating teacher.

Most of the questions raised concerning the desirability of general supervision lie in the area of secondary education, for it is at this level that the problem most generally occurs. Elementary supervision is nearly always general in nature since elementary classrooms normally do not lend themselves to specialized supervision.

As Pfeiffer noted, the use of general supervisors might lessen the possibilities of conflict since the areas of competency of the two supervisory personnel differ. In practice, however, this does not always seem to be the case. Most classroom teachers have sufficient convictions as to how one should teach

[3] Robert T. Pfeiffer, Editor, The College Supervisor--Conflict and Challenge, 43rd Yearbook, The Association for Student Teaching, 1964, p. 13.

that conflict in method could occur just as often in general supervisory programs as in any other. The supervisory approach of the college representative, therefore, still needs to recognize basic principles of cooperative endeavor. Interestingly enough, there is seldom conflict in determining ways in which the student teacher's development should proceed. Cooperating teachers seem quite willing to let the college supervisor assume this initiative and, indeed, seem to welcome it.

Specialized college supervision. The pattern of having college supervisors who are subject specialists often finds various provisions made in the selection of those who are to do the supervisory job. Some liberal arts colleges and smaller institutions delegate the supervisory job to subject specialists from academic departments rather than from those affiliated with Education departments. Unless considerable caution is followed, this practice can contribute little to the improvement of the student teacher. Most academicians in college departments are woefully uninformed about the public school and its problems as well as the public school pupil. This is not an indictment of this group, for their professional preparation has not included this facet in their formal education nor in their experience. Granted that many classroom teachers could profit academically from association with academic specialists, it still remains that the primary function of student teaching is the development of the college student into a classroom teacher.

There are some institutions who are fortunate enough to have members of academic departments who are also competent in professional education. Such supervisors may provide excellent supervision for prospective teachers and provide an excellent source of college supervisory personnel.

Larger institutions who have major teacher education commitments sometimes utilize specialized supervisory personnel who are equally competent in academic fields and in professional education. As members of the appropriate Education department, they assume the supervisory role in a somewhat different relationship than the general supervisor although there is also much similarity in their responsibilities.

In contrast with the general supervisor, the specialist often becomes more directly involved in actual planning with the student teacher and is more familiar with available materials in the particular field of teaching and with specific approaches to teaching certain subjects. He is, therefore, able to assume a consultant role with the cooperating teacher.

One must recognize that, as a subject specialist, the college supervisor may create more insecurity in the mind of the classroom teacher. His approach and personality must be such that he shows respect for the classroom teacher and recognizes that he, too, is a specialist. The human relationship factor is perhaps more critical in this pattern of supervision than in the general supervisory approach.

Because the specialized supervisor often spends more time individually with the student teacher, particularly in planning lessons, the number of students which he is expected to serve is often less than in general supervisory programs. The added time and fewer student teachers both contribute to the effectiveness of the specialized supervisor. He is often in a position to be of more help to the student teacher since he can offer constructive suggestions in both academic and methodological areas.

It is difficult to ascertain which of the two prevailing patterns of supervision is preferable. Given the appropriate personality, it would appear that the specialized supervisor who can make the greatest contribution in both academic and educational areas might be superior to the generalist. The individual competency of the supervisor and his perception of the supervisory role are variables, however, which may affect the effectiveness of his supervision more than the designation of special or general supervisor.

ADDITIONAL REFERENCES

Combs, Arthur W., *The Professional Education of Teachers*, Boston: Allyn and Bacon, Inc., 1965.

Edwards, Helen E., *Building Good Relationships: A Major Role of the College Supervisor*, Bulletin No. 16, The Association for Student Teaching, 1961.

Haines, Aleyne C., *Guiding the Student Teaching Process in Elementary Education*, Chicago: Rand McNally and Company, 1960.

Lewis, Claudia and Charlotte Winsor, "Supervising the Beginning Teacher," *Educational Leadership*, 17:137-141, December, 1959.

Pfeiffer, Robert T., Editor, *The College Supervisor--Conflict and Challenge*, 43rd Yearbook, The Association for Student Teaching, 1964.

Sharpe, Donald M., "An Analysis of Teaching Load for College Supervisors of Secondary Student Teaching--Indiana State College," *The Teachers College Journal*, 35:42-45, November, 1963.

Steeves, Frank L., *Issues in Student Teaching*, New York: The Odyssey Press, Inc., 1963.

Taylor, Gem K. and Jack W. Fields, "Problems Confronting the College Coordinator in an Off-Campus Student Teaching Program," *Peabody Journal of Education*, 41:308-311, March, 1964.

Chapter V

The Student Teaching Experience

There was decided tension in her throat as Nancy White walked up to the front door of Garfield Junior High School. It was the first day of student teaching She had visited the school before, of course, shortly after she had learned of her student teaching assignment last May. At that time she had met Mrs. Allen, her cooperating teacher, and the school principal, Mr. Jackson. Then, however, she was merely a visitor--now she was a teacher.

She had found Mrs. Allen to be a pleasant person in her early forties. She had a quiet, patient way of working with her pupils and was obviously a successful teacher because she used her quiet personality to advantage. The pupils appeared to like her very much; she seemed to enjoy teaching them. A smile of commendation from Mrs. Allen was all the reward the pupils desired. Nancy had noticed that the junior high youngsters were much more orderly and better behaved in Mrs. Allen's room than they were in the hallway, although the atmosphere was free and easy.

Mrs. Allen taught English and social studies to the seventh grade. She had two classes in each field, a study hall, and a free period. These were the classes in which Nancy was to observe and work.

Entering the building, Nancy headed for the principal's office. The secretary recognized her name when Nancy introduced herself and immediately ushered her into the principal's office. Mr. Jackson seemed glad to see her again and expressed the hope that Nancy would enjoy her semester as a member of the school staff. He showed her a cloakroom where she could keep her wraps in his outer office.

Since it was the first day of school and he was very busy, Mr. Jackson asked his secretary to take Nancy to Mrs. Allen's room. He asked Nancy to come back to see him during the afternoon or after school when he would have more time to talk with her.

Mrs. Allen greeted her warmly. She, too, was busy getting ready for the first day of school. After asking Nancy if she were ready to begin work, Mrs. Allen gave her a list of names, asking her to write them on the chalkboard. While Nancy wrote, Mrs. Allen explained that the names were those of the first two classes in the morning since the same pupils were in her English and social studies classes. She pointed out that the pupils came from different elementary schools and that the names would help them get acquainted with one another.

As soon as the job was completed, Mrs. Allen expressed satisfaction and indicated that they were now ready for the pupils. She explained that they would report as soon as the opening day assembly program was over.

While they waited for the class, Mrs. Allen showed Nancy the textbooks which were being used in her classes and gave her copies for her own use. She showed her the curriculum guide for the city schools and suggested that Nancy take it home with her to familiarize herself with the work which might be done during the semester of student teaching. Mrs. Allen pointed out that Nancy would profit most from observing the classes for a few days, becoming acquainted with the pupils, becoming familiar with the school routine, and perhaps working with small groups of pupils on occasion. After a few days, Mrs. Allen said, they would decide together on exactly what teaching and other duties Nancy would later assume.

A rumble of footsteps broke the silence and came nearer. Through the door came the class They settled into convenient seats, obviously somewhat excited about the beginning of school. When Mrs. Allen rose from behind her desk, the noise subsided. Mrs. Allen spoke quietly with a smile. "Good morning, boys and girls. My name is Mrs. Allen--I am your English and social studies teacher. I want you to meet Miss White. Miss White is assigned to help me teach your classes for this first semester. Not every class is lucky enough to have two teachers working with it. I know we shall have a pleasant year working together."

Nancy rose as she was introduced, smiled and said, "Good morning, class." Her knees were shaking, she was very self-conscious, but she was beginning to feel like a teacher.

Obviously, every student teaching assignment will not fall into the exact pattern as the one just described, but there are implications in Nancy's experience which will provide the beginnings of a good student teaching semester. She had visited the school previously; she reported to the principal and was made to feel welcome; the teacher had something in mind for her to do which made her feel that she was contributing something worthwhile; she was provided materials to give her an overview of the semester's work; she knew what she was to do first--observe, get to know pupils, get acquainted with the work of the class; she was introduced in a way which made her feel a part of the teaching staff.

A look at the student teacher

The student teacher comes to the classroom assignment with mixed emotions. He has all the anxieties which usually accompany any new experience, while realizing at the same time that his student teaching performance is a critical aspect of his teacher education program. He is eager to teach and wants to do a good job; yet he is apprehensive about his capabilities and his acceptance by the pupils, the cooperating teacher, and the school.

He must be made to feel that he is welcome. Many cooperating teachers are not aware of the highly emotional state of most beginning student teachers and the insecurity they feel. Often casual comments are misinterpreted by student teachers because of their emotional state, and they get an erroneous conception of their position or acceptance in the classroom situation.

The student teacher does not come to the classroom as one who knows how to teach. If such were the case, student teaching would be unnecessary. He does come with a background of content and theory sufficient to enable him to learn something about teaching. He is ready to learn and after a reasonably satisfactory student teaching experience will have learned about teaching to the point where he can assume major responsibility in the classroom.

Student teachers themselves often do not realize their role in student teaching. They feel that they must emulate the cooperating teacher and feel inferior when their teaching falls short of this goal. This often prevents their developing individualized teaching approaches of their own. Everyone involved, including the student teacher, must realize that the college student is in a learning situation if the prospective teacher is to succeed.

Building success in student teaching

The student teaching experience begins the first moment that the student teacher enters the school building. He begins to form impressions of the school, the pupils, the teachers, and teaching in general. It is the responsibility of the building principal and the cooperating teacher to see that these impressions are wholesome and such that the student teacher may build upon them.

The actual teaching experience is a gradual transition from dependency to initiative. The rate at which the student teacher advances along the continuum to independence depends upon his ability to understand and interpret his experiences and the background which he brings to the classroom. During the first few weeks of student teaching, the student teacher is very dependent upon the cooperating teacher. He may be alert enough to see things he might do, but he is often hesitant to volunteer his efforts until he knows the latitude he will be given by the teacher to whom he is assigned. The cooperating teacher must recognize that student teaching involves the total role of the teacher and is not confined to the classroom alone. He must be aware of the many learning opportunities available in the school and of the student teacher's alertness in profiting from them. The broader the experience, the better the prospective teacher will fit into the teaching role in his first job.

The first few weeks of student teaching are customarily involved in acquainting the student teacher with the situation to which he is assigned. This includes meeting the staff members and administrative officials and becoming familiar with their functions in the school program, particularly those with whom he will come in contact in his teaching duties. Special experiences may be provided, if needed, with such personnel as librarians, guidance counselors, audio-visual coordinators, etc. The author well remembers the impressions made upon a student teacher who had a rather sheltered background by having her spend a day with the attendance officer in a large city.

Orientation to the student teaching situation is not a process which is accomplished in a day or two. It takes considerable time for the student teacher to know the pupils, the community, and the school well. It is much more dangerous to rush the orientation of prospective teachers than to take too long for the task, although extremes of either kind should be avoided.

During the period of orientation, student teachers should be given opportunities to contribute something to the on-going activities of the classroom. Since they approach student teaching with eagerness to teach, too much delay in providing them with specific things to do in the classroom prolongs their uncertainty and, indeed, does much to kill the enthusiasm which they bring to the experience. Successful orientation requires a planned approach rather than "catch as catch can". Learning is as much an active process for student teachers as it is for pupils in the classroom and should be planned and provided for just as carefully. This is an important part of the cooperating teacher's responsibilities.

It is axiomatic in teaching that the teacher must know as much as possible about the pupils in his charge. The student teaching participant must, therefore, learn about the pupils in his classes. Cumulative records, discussion with the cooperating teacher, and direct observation of the pupils all contribute to this end. One of the important aspects of orientation to the community is the familiarization with the socio-economic backgrounds of the students attending any particular school.

Included in the orientation to the school is familiarization with special instructional tools available such as audio-visual equipment, library facilities, curriculum guides, and special programs of the school.

During the early conferences with the cooperating teacher and the college supervisor, the student teacher should participate in developing the overall plans for his student teaching experience. Tentative plans should be made concerning the approximate time when various aspects of the teaching role will be assumed by the student teacher along with the areas he will cover in his teaching. Such plans should be cooperatively developed, taking into consideration the student teacher's background, special interests, general ability, and the goals of the cooperating teacher for the class. It should be emphasized that all developmental plans should be tentative since adjustments must be made in the light of the student teacher's progress. If the student teacher has some general understanding of what he is expected to do, however, he has more knowledge of the total picture and is much more secure in his new role. No one can perform well in a situation where he never knows what he will be doing next.

Stated briefly, *the student teacher should have orientation to everything the teacher needs to know in order to do an effective job of teaching*.

Early assignments given the student teacher should be clearly defined with definite instructions. A common error is to assume that the student teacher knows what to do when he is asked to complete a given task when actually there is considerable doubt in his mind, simple as the job may seem to the cooperating teacher.

Working the student teacher into the activities of the class gradually must be carefully planned. It will not occur naturally without the cooperating teacher's making provision for it. The confidence and respect which the cooperating teacher shows toward the student teacher will be reflected in the pupils. The way in which the teacher utilizes the student teacher in his planning will do much to set the proper pattern in this respect.

By gradually involving the student teacher in his own teaching, the cooperating teacher will soon have him to the point where he can assume major teaching responsibilities and grow less and less dependent upon the guidance of the classroom teacher.

Initial duties of the student teacher should be those in which he can succeed and which he can do without a great deal of planning. There are many simple tasks which are part of the teaching role which could be assigned to and performed by the student teacher. Some of these are routine and administrative--others involve working relationships with pupils. By no means, however, should the student teacher be thrust into the position of teaching a class during the first few days of his assignment, although such practice is reported by student teachers far too often. There is ample time in the student teaching experience for this to be a gradual induction.

Among the minor teaching duties which might involve the student teacher in the early days of his assignment are:

checking attendance
putting material on the chalkboard
recording grades
giving vocabulary or spelling words
calling on pupils for oral reports
helping pupils plan and prepare bulletin boards
collecting and distributing papers or materials
helping work with pupil committees
monitoring tests in class
giving make-up examinations

All of these should be conducted under the close supervision of the cooperating teacher. As the student grows in confidence and ability in these tasks, he begins to desire more responsibilities and soon reaches the point where he can be given a lesson to plan and present on his own.

Perhaps a word of caution should be included. The student teacher is not in his assignment to serve as a "flunky" for the cooperating teacher and should not be exploited into unprofitable clerical and paper-grading chores. If such activities can serve educational purposes for the student teacher, they should be included in his realm of responsibilities. They can be supported only in educational terms, however. This should not be interpreted to imply that student teachers should be of no help to the cooperating teacher but rather that moderation should be the watchword.

One of the most common questions asked by cooperating teachers is, "When will he take over the class?" One frequently hears reference to "two weeks of observation and then teach." Such practice, although fairly common, is not conducive to the best student teaching performance. If the experience is to be a gradual growth from dependency to initiative, the abrupt break from a passive to an active role fails to follow this prescription. The transition is made in the best situations in such a way that the pupils in the class are nearly unaware that the teaching responsibility has shifted from the classroom teacher to the student teacher.

Another questionable practice which is quite common is to assign the student teacher, during his early days, to work with pupils who are remedial cases or who are so advanced that individual instruction would profit them. While it is commendable to have the prospective teacher work with small groups on occasion, pupils who need special help are often in need of more skillful instruction than the student teacher can provide at this early stage of his development professionally.

Once the student teacher has reached a point where he can assume the teaching role, he should have a chance to teach for a continuous period of time. This does not necessarily mean that the student must continue until the end of the semester or the end of the student teaching assignment. It might be more judicious to have him complete a unit or part of a unit with a break following where he might again observe the cooperating teacher with the same class, followed by another period of teaching. There is some evidence that observation after having taught is more profitable than that made earlier.

Some cooperating teachers have found it valuable to provide time during the school day when the student teacher might be free to utilize his time as he sees fit. This might include time for planning, paper-grading, observing in other classes, or study in the areas in which he is teaching. Such practice is particularly valuable when the student teacher is involved in teaching several classes or when his outside time is taken up with college courses.

There is a temptation for school administrators to use student teachers as substitute teachers. Most colleges frown on this practice. This is not the purpose of student teaching and, in most instances, the student teacher is not competent to move into a strange class and assume instruction. It is probably true that as he nears the completion of his student teaching, such an assignment might be a real learning situation for him, but fear of abuse has kept most colleges from encouraging such practice. If no substitute can be found for situations which arise unexpectedly, some administrators leave the student teacher in charge of the class with which he is familiar and have the cooperating teacher assume the substitute role. While this is probably better than having the student teacher substitute, it is not often welcomed by cooperating teachers. Extensive use of such a practice might well result in a great reluctance on the part of cooperating teachers to accept student teachers.

There is no formula for determining how much teaching the college student should be expected to do. Some colleges prefer to limit the experience to one or two classes at the secondary level or to a very few areas at any one time in elementary classes. Others expect the student teacher to do considerable teaching for an extended period of time. It would appear that before the student teaching period has been completed, there should be an opportunity for the student teacher to do a full day of teaching, if possible, although such experience should be confined to a relatively brief period. It is usually better for the student teacher to teach fewer areas at any one time and to do well that which he attempts.

The cooperating teacher should always be alert to ways in which the student teacher might learn more about the school and its pupils. School social affairs, extra-curricular activities, professional meetings, and committee work all offer such opportunities. Student teachers do not feel free to attend many such functions unless they have been told that they would be welcome. Faculty meetings, P. T. A. affairs, parent conferences and the like offer valuable opportunities for expanding the scope of the student teacher's learning experience.

Del Popolo sums up the student teaching experience in four basic principles:

1. The student teacher should be gradually inducted into the responsibilities of actual teaching.
2. The plan of inducting the student teacher will then be from the easy to the difficult, from the simple to the complex, from observation to participation, and to long-term teaching.
3. The student teacher is to be thought of as a distinct personality, capable of growth, sensitive to success and failure, and deserving of help and consideration.
4. The student-teaching activities should be conducted in as natural and typical situation as possible.[1]

Problems of student teachers

Since each student teaching experience is a unique one, no two student teachers will have the same problems throughout the assignment. There are some areas in common in which

[1] Joseph A. DelPopolo, "Experiences a Student Teacher Should Have," The Journal of Teacher Education, March, 1960, p. 76-77.

student teachers seem to have difficulty, however. The extent to which they need nelp in coping with these problems varies, but the teacher working with student teachers should be sensitive to these areas and should be alert in providing help in solving them if necessary.

1. *Problems of pupil control and behavior.* Before beginning student teaching, the prospective teacher is probably more concerned with this area than any other. He is often apprehensive about "discipline" problems and wonders about his capability in controlling pupils. In actual practice this does not prove to be a problem if the student teacher inherits a climate conducive to learning and if lesson plans are well-made. The student teacher who is unsure of what he should do next often loses the class control and respect and problems do then occur. The necessity of good planning should be stressed not only from the standpoint of good teaching but also from the standpoint of organized classroom control.

It should be emphasized to the student teacher that his relationships with pupils must be that of a teacher and not as a "friend to all and a brother to every other scout." The age differential is so slight at the secondary level that pupils may attempt to get too close to the student teacher. Oftentimes elementary student teachers tend to "mother" the elementary school child too much. There must be an aura of respect if instruction is to be successful.

Young ladies have additional problems, particularly if they are personable and attractive. Seldom are these difficult to manage--a sense of humor and a businesslike attitude usually results in the proper relationship.

The student teacher should be informed early of the latitude he has with respect to maintaining good classroom control. The cooperating teacher should lay out the ground rules and support the student teacher in whatever he attempts. Under no circumstances should the student teacher become involved in administering corporal punishment or trying to cope with very serious disciplinary problems alone. These should be handled by persons with more authority than the student teacher.

2. *Motivating pupil interest.* This problem is a common one for experienced teachers; it becomes more critical for the student teacher because of his lack of experience.

Much help can be given by the cooperating teacher by explaining why he proceeds in particular ways in his teaching. Joint-planning and study of projected plans of the classroom teacher with emphasis on motivational aspects of putting the plans into operation will give insights into this problem area. Paralleling this are evaluative conferences over the plans of both the cooperating teacher and the student teacher, looking at the successes and failures of the motivational techniques utilized. Principles of motivation can best be learned by seeing them in action; demonstration remains a choice way of teaching.

The student teacher must learn that the motivation of pupils depends on their understanding and acceptance of the purposes of the lesson. He must know that the procedures he selects and the materials he uses must be sufficiently interesting and profitable that pupils will remain interested in learning that which is intended.

By making learning an active process for the pupils and by using proper pupil-teacher planning, the student teacher lessens motivation problems and tastes success. Basic to all of these is the kind of personality which makes pupils enjoy working with and for the teacher.

A variety of teaching methods enables the student teacher to maintain an attentive climate so long as the methods are commensurate with the abilities of the class and the objectives of the lesson. He should be challenged on both of these criteria as he develops his teaching plans.

The student teacher must learn the importance of making assignments in a way which will motivate the pupils to complete them. This is not an easy task and requires thought and advanced planning just as much as any other part of the lesson.

3. *Adapting instruction to individual differences*. This persistent problem of teaching is no less a problem for student teachers than for others. Its solution depends upon recognizing differences which exist, knowing the variety of instructional materials available, and being familiar with techniques of grouping and individualized instruction which attempt to provide ways of promoting pupil growth. The student teacher must start early in identifying specific abilities and needs and will need much help in his planning to adapt his instruction toward meeting discernible differences.

The cooperating teacher can call the student teacher's attention to methods employed by other teachers whom the student observes and attempt to make him aware of what he is observing.

4. *Questioning*. Until one has had the experience of selecting appropriate questions to ask of pupils, he is not aware of the difficulty some student teachers have in this regard. In his early teaching, the student teacher has not yet learned to think on his feet and often stumbles in searching for good questions in a class recitation period. He often needs help in posing thought-provoking questions or in deriving questions which point to basic understandings rather than rote recall of the textbook.

It is suggested that early lesson plans include some specific questions over pertinent parts of the lesson to guide the student teacher in conducting class discussion. The cooperating teacher must remind the student to get participation from all and to stimulate questions from pupils. He must learn to pose questions which are clear and understandable, which lead to the response desired, and which cause pupils to think.

It is only through experience with proper guidance that the student teacher is able to develop questions which function properly and carry the class to the desired conclusions. He must learn to address questions to the entire class, to make them self-explanatory, and to make his questioning move in a developmental way to logical ends.

5. *Budgeting time and controlling tempo*. The student teacher must, through experience, learn to pace his teaching efforts so that the pupils learn what is intended in as economical way as possible. Student teachers are often amazed at the timing of their first efforts as a major teaching task. They do not know how much can reasonably be accomplished in a given time period. For this reason, if for no other, the initial plans of the student teacher must be carefully checked. Some cooperating teachers have the student teacher designate approximately how much time should be devoted to specific parts of the lesson to enable the student to pace the lesson properly. It must be emphasized that such time allocations must be flexible and that the student teacher must make certain that the pupils understand what is being taught before moving on to new parts of the lesson.

The same principle applies to long-range or unit planning. This prevents the student teacher from following tangents or spending too much time on unimportant details.

The student teacher must also budget his time outside of actual teaching so that he has the necessary time available for planning and auxiliary duties which may be involved in the student teaching experience. He should be encouraged to minimize his social and outside activities during student teaching, for this experience is time-consuming if done properly. This is particularly true if the student is carrying additional classes at college or is involved in part-time employment. Too great commitments will be reflected in poor preparation and poor teaching, which will in turn affect the student's ability to secure a choice teaching position after graduation.

ADDITIONAL REFERENCES

Batchelder, Howard T., Maurice McGlasson, and Raleigh Schorling, *Student Teaching in Secondary Schools*, New York: McGraw Hill Book Co., Inc., 1964.

Carroll, Margaret, Dorothy M. McGeoch, and Carl W. Proehl, Editors, *Four Went To Teach*, 35th Yearbook, The Association for Student Teaching, 1956.

DelPopolo, Joseph A., "Experiences a Student Teacher Should Have," *The Journal of Teacher Education*, 11:75-78, March, 1960.

Devor, John W., *The Experience of Student Teaching*, New York: The Macmillan Company, 1964.

Greene, Gwynn A., *Problem Situations in Student Teaching*, Bureau of Publications, Teachers College, Columbia University, 1959.

Henry, Marvin A., "The Relationship of Difficulties of Student Teachers to Selected Aspects of the Professional Sequence of Education," *The Teachers College Journal*, 35:47-49, November, 1963.

Thompson, Michael L., "Identifying Anxieties Experienced by Student Teachers," *The Journal of Teacher Education*, 14:435-439, December, 1963.

Wingo, G. Max and Raleigh Schorling, *Elementary School Student Teaching*, New York: McGraw Hill Book Co., Inc., 1960.

Chapter VI

Working With Student Teachers

Working with a successful student teacher can be a source of pleasure and enjoyment for a cooperating teacher. The knowledge that one is helping a young person make a contribution as important as teaching provides nourishment to the altruistic attitude of teachers. Success in student teaching, however, does not come automatically. It involves much work and study as well as raw material capable of being molded into the competent classroom teacher. Many factors and many activities must be involved in making the transition from college student to teacher.

Readiness for student teaching

There are as many differences among student teachers as there are among the pupils in any classroom. They come to the student teaching experience with varying degrees of readiness for the teaching role. It must be assumed that their selection for student teaching by the college assures a reasonable degree of content knowledge and professional preparation. The professional zeal, emotional stability, receptivity to suggestions, and previous contacts with children and youth which provide the readiness to assume teaching responsibilities will differ greatly. One of the more difficult jobs of the cooperating teacher is to develop a sensitivity to these many aspects of the teaching personality so that he may plan the developmental phases of student teaching for each particular student teacher.

Illustrative of the differences which are obvious are the following brief sketches of three student teachers:

> *Janet Adams*, age 22, is the only child of well-to-do parents, both college graduates. She has traveled widely although not outside continental United States. Janet is attractive and sure of herself. She is always well-groomed and wears expensive clothes. She has made good grades in college, although not outstanding in this respect. She

has had no contacts with children except for occasional "visits with my young cousins." Janet is engaged and plans on marriage upon graduation next June. It is doubtful if she will ever teach, but the teaching certificate will be a good "insurance policy."

George Davis, age 25, is a sincere, hard-working young man. He has served two years in military service and started to college late. His financial assistance from home is limited; consequently, he has had to work at part-time jobs while going to college. His grades have been satisfactory although he has had to work hard for them. He has two younger brothers and one older sister who is married and did not attend college. George has worked at a boys' camp during two summers and is employed part-time as a life-guard in the local YMCA while completing his college work. His only plans at present are to "complete college and teach."

Mary James, an average student, got married at the end of her junior year of college. She and her husband are both in school with some financial assistance from both families, although at times it is difficult to make ends meet. She is interested in keeping house in their small apartment and in completing her elementary teaching certificate. Mary comes from a family with a moderate income but her mother is an invalid. She plans on teaching while her husband completes his work for a law degree, then she hopes to become a full-time housewife and mother.

With these many differences so obvious in background and motivation, one can only surmise the great differences present in other ways which require considerable exploration to ascertain.

As one works with many student teachers, he readily observes that some student teachers have an intense interest in teaching and are eager to assume teaching duties as quickly as possible while others are less eager or even afraid of being given some responsibilities. Readiness for teaching is extremely complex and difficult to ascertain. There are a few observable factors, however, which may help the cooperating teacher and campus supervisor to determine the extent of readiness of the student teacher if they are alert to them and provide the opportunities for the readiness factors to assert themselves.

One clue to student teaching readiness lies in the kind of questions raised by the student teacher as he observes the cooperating teacher and other teachers while they are teaching. As a general rule, the student teacher who asks few questions is not as ready for assuming teaching duties as one who is searching for answers. One must also consider the kind of questions asked by the student. Questions concerned with minute details or extraneous matters usually indicate a lack of depth in understanding the many implications of teaching. On the other hand, questions which get at basic issues or are more penetrating into the daily work of the class as well as long-range goals suggest readiness for moving into more complex activities.

Another indication of readiness is the student teacher's ability to see things which he might do without being asked. The initiative shown in this way indicates the grasp which the student has of the situation. Parallel to this is the quality of the work undertaken by the student teacher. The more thoroughly he carries out the various tasks undertaken, both those for which he volunteers and those assigned to him, the more likely he is ready to assume greater responsibilities.

The student teacher's emotional stability is also a factor in his readiness for teaching. Most student teachers are nervous at first, but the more mature overcome this quickly and easily. The cooperating teacher should watch carefully the relationship of the student teacher to the pupils and note the poise which the student teacher displays in his working relationships.

Such overt actions by the student teacher as being late to school, avoiding conferences, finding excuses for not doing assigned jobs, and doing incomplete work are obvious indications of a lack of proper readiness to participate in the teaching role.

The cooperating teacher can foster the growth of readiness in the student teacher by using good judgment in the kind of tasks assigned and by providing opportunities for the student teacher to volunteer for various activities. He can also provide opportunities for the student teacher to ask questions. He can sincerely commend the student teacher when a job has been completed satisfactorily. A show of confidence on the part of the cooperating teacher gives encouragement and security to the student teacher.

If the cooperating teacher detects a lack of readiness on the part of the student teacher to the point where he seriously questions the student's ability to participate in the student teaching experience, he should communicate with the college supervisor as quickly as possible. Joint action by the two supervisors may eliminate a potential unpleasant experience for all parties, including the student teacher, and may, indeed, salvage one who is not yet ready to assume the role of classroom teacher.

Observation

Since the early days of student teaching are spent in considerable observation, the cooperating teacher must take the initiative in making these observations profitable. Observation which is unguided and not evaluated often proves to be a waste of time. Students need to know what to look for and how to interpret what they see.

Not only in the early days of the experience but also throughout the student teaching assignment there should be opportunities provided for observing both the cooperating teacher and other teachers in the building or the school district. The principal can be of great help in facilitating arrangements for other observations outside the cooperating teacher's classroom. It is necessary to provide a routine in making such arrangements in advance. Most teachers do not object to having student teachers observe in their classrooms, but they usually want to know a few days in advance of any planned visitation.

If observation can be structured so that only a few important areas are to be studied at any one time, it will be more meaningful to the college student. If the student teacher has to look for many things at the same time, he may end up with little specific knowledge to help him. Proper provision for maximum benefits from observation must be made for every observation period.

In guiding the student's observations, the following questions might be raised with him, both before and following the classroom visit:

1. THE CLASSROOM

   A. What motivational aspects do you find with respect to display materials?
   B. How does the classroom environment contribute to pupil learning?
   C. What evidence do you find of pupil participation in bulletin board displays?
   D. What is the seating arrangement?
   E. How is the room environment related to what is being studied?

2. THE TEACHER

   A. How does the teacher promote good inter-personal relationships among pupils?
   B. What specific things does the teacher do to build rapport with the pupils?
   C. What evidences can you find of "democratic" classroom procedures?
   D. Does the teacher utilize pupils in routine administrative and housekeeping duties?
   E. How does the teacher begin and close the lesson?
   F. What instructional materials and teaching aids are used to supplement the textbook?
   G. How does the teacher maintain pupil interest and participation?

3. THE PUPIL

   A. How enthusiastic are the pupils about the lesson?
   B. Is the class grouped by ability or in any other way?
   C. What differences among the pupils can you identify?
   D. What is the socio-economic background of the pupils?
   E. How do the pupils participate in planning the work of the class for this and subsequent lessons?
   F. Do you detect any pupils who appear to have special problems of adjustment, ability, or inter-personal relationships?
   G. Is pupil participation evenly distributed or confined to only a few pupils?

4. THE LESSON

   A. What indications can you find of relating the lesson to other courses or previous content?
   B. How does the teacher conduct class discussion to insure participation by all?
   C. Can you identify any objectives of the teacher other than mastery of the content studied?
   D. How frequently does the teacher summarize pertinent points?
   E. How are assignments developed?
   F. How are individual differences provided for in giving assignments and in conducting the lesson?
   G. How much outside work is expected of the pupils?
   H. How much of the lesson is review and how much is new work?
   I. How is class drill made interesting?
   J. What type of questions does the teacher ask?

It is not expected that the student teacher will attempt to find answers to all of these questions in any one observation period. Rather, one or two of these areas only will be concentrated upon in any given observation visit. The cooperating teacher or principal can assure that the student teacher will profit from his visitations by making arrangements for the student to observe teachers who excel in the particular areas under consideration. It helps also to notify the teacher who is to be observed of the specific points the student teacher is interested in observing.

No observation is complete without careful and thorough follow-up through discussion and interpretation with the student teacher. Only in this way can the student teacher learn to analyze and evaluate his own teaching proficiency.

Guiding child study

The student teacher needs to know his pupils specifically and as much as possible about the characteristics of the age-group which he expects to teach. Since the student teaching experience often provides him with his first long-term opportunity to work with and to study children, much can be learned if full advantage is taken of the many opportunities present. His study is naturally concentrated on the particular pupils with whom he is working, but if the classes with whom he works are not atypical, he can draw some valid generalizations about children of the same age-group.

The cumulative records of pupils offer much information of which the student teacher may avail himself. This cannot be done by merely having him examine the records, however. He must have guidance if he is to interpret the records accurately and profitably. Much of the general background information is as obvious to the student teacher as to anyone else, but implications of this information for his teaching need to be explained and examined with him. The interpretation of standardized test scores will often be a new experience in which he will need some help. Student teachers are often unfamiliar with specific tests and with such reporting devices as norms, percentiles, standard scores, etc. It should be emphasized to the student teacher that the records contain privileged communication and information and that he must use them only in a professional way.

It is often valuable to have the student teacher talk with the guidance counselor and the school psychologist if such personnel are available. In this way he can get additional insights into children as well as equip himself to take advantage of such specialized personnel in his own teaching.

There are occasions when a detailed case study might be valuable. If the student teacher appears to be particularly weak in his understanding of children or if he has a "problem" pupil in his class who needs careful understanding, the preparation of a case study might prove very helpful to the student teacher. Although some supervisors have all student teachers prepare case studies as a matter of routine, the time and effort which go into such a project, if it is done well, are such that the time might better be spent in other ways for some student teachers. This is particularly true if he has had such an experience in previous professional courses. It is important, however, that he become acquainted with sources of pertinent information about pupils. As with many other techniques, the case study has its good uses and its bad and must be used judiciously.

In place of a case study, some cooperating teachers have the student teacher prepare a short descriptive paragraph on each of the pupils in his class or classes, summarizing pertinent information derived from the cumulative records, teacher conferences, and from other sources. These are often helpful to the student teacher in his teaching as well as in providing additional understanding which he needs.

As problems arise concerning specific pupils, the cooperating teacher can offer guidance by asking pointed questions of the student teacher, attempting to get the student to ascertain the focus of the problem rather than by providing the answer for him.

Conferences with student teachers

Frequent conferences between the student teacher and the cooperating teacher are essential if real help is to be provided for the prospective teacher. It is through the conference that the cooperating teacher makes his greatest contribution to the student teacher's growth. Constructive conferences must be built upon common understandings and goals. This would imply that early in the student teaching experience the cooperating teacher and the student teacher become well-acquainted professionally and understand not only the goals of the student teaching program but also the goals for the instruction of the pupils to be taught. The better the job done by the college in providing the cooperating teacher with information about the student teacher, the more quickly the teacher can begin to develop the specific student teaching experiences. The following pages illustrate the personal data sheet provided by one institution for this purpose and the biographical sketch written by a student.

It is important that a regular time and place be determined for conferences in order that both parties may be prepared. It is true that many opportunities arise during the school day for frequent short "on the spot" suggestions, but these do not take the place of the need for longer, planned deliberations and work sessions. Finding time for conferences sometimes presents a problem, particularly in part-time student teaching assignments. It is not asking too much for the cooperating teacher to insist upon conferences with the student teacher at specific times even though the student teacher may have to return to the school at a time convenient to the cooperating teacher. Conferences are so important that a good student teaching experience cannot be provided without them.

MIAMI UNIVERSITY
Oxford, Ohio
Confidential Information Blank For Student Teaching

Name ____
last first middle

Home address ____

Teaching areas for which you will be certified: ____________________

____

EDUCATIONAL BACKGROUND:

High school from which you were graduated __________ Year __________

Colleges attended other than Miami ______________________________

Honors received at high school or college ______________________

____

____

PERSONAL EXPERIENCES:

Summarize briefly any experience you have had with children and youth, i.e., teaching church school, boy or girl scouts, etc.:

____

____

____

____

Summarize briefly any work experience you have had, including summer employment:

____

____

____

On the average, how many hours per week have you worked while in college? ____________________

Kind of work done while in college ______________________________

____

____

FAMILY BACKGROUND:

Father's name in full ______________________________
last first middle

Occupation ______________________________

Mother's name in full ______________________________
last first middle

Occupation, if any, in addition to homemaking ______________

Number of children in family older than yourself: Boys ____ Girls ____

Number of children in family younger than yourself: Boys ____ Girls ____

RECREATIONAL AND HOBBY INTERESTS: list all those activities in which you have engaged, both in and out of school, indicating your special favorites.

____

____

____

SCHOOL AND COMMUNITY ACTIVITIES: give the nature and extent of your participation and responsibility in church, camp, recreation, youth organizations and school activities. Indicate those from which you received the most satisfaction and benefit with reasons for your choice.

____

____

____

____

Write a brief autobiographical sketch. Include those influences that have helped shape your development, experiences that have seemed most worth-while, reasons why you decided to become a teacher, your life's ambitions, any big problems you have faced, and difficulties you have overcome. Use the remainder of this paper and the back side of this sheet if necessary.

AUTOBIOGRAPHICAL SKETCH: Cathryn Lewis

There are many reasons why I want to become a teacher. Although it seems impossible to narrow down all of the circumstances which cause a person to want to enter a particular field, I can determine the most attractive element in teaching for me. That is the opportunity to be creative. I realize that there are boundaries to be observed in teaching; however, the alternative fields which I have considered for my life's work are definitely more limiting. In these areas, one must work for years to acquire an executive position which would allow an amount of personal freedom in planning and executing equal to that to be found in teaching.

All of my past activities have been influenced by this desire to create. On the campus I have served as president and vice-president of my sorority and have enjoyed working closely with groups as well as initiating and carrying through various programs. I participated in activities offering similar opportunities in high school where I was captain of the drill team, managing editor of the paper, and president of the Methodist Youth Fellowship. Realizing that extra-curricular activities are a vital and time-consuming part of my education, I have tried to keep a reasonable balance between them and my academic responsibilities. In high school I was a member of the National Honor Society and received the DAR good citizenship award. At college I have been elected to Sigma Delta Pi, Spanish honorary fraternity, and have been on the Dean's list frequently.

In my spare time I am addicted to all sports, particularly golf and swimming and greatly enjoy playing bridge.

I have lived in Colorado and in Indiana and enjoyed both places very much. I have a particular fondness for the mountains and hope to return to them some day. This fondness is shared by my sister, who is two years younger than I, and my father who is a geologist and is probably responsible for our interest.

I have had little experience with children other than babysitting. I have worked as a waitress in a summer resort and have done clerical work in an insurance office for two summers. I hope to improve my Spanish by attending school next summer in Mexico.

I am looking forward eagerly to my student teaching and to several years of working with young people in the classroom.

If conferences are helpful, everyone concerned will look forward to them. They should be well-planned and purposeful. There is no need to meet just for the sake of holding a conference; each one should serve some useful and needed purpose.

Conferences should be constructive and should be cooperative. This does not mean that mistakes should not be mentioned, but they should be discussed with an eye toward profiting from them. Consistent negative comments will not only discourage the student teacher but will cause him to avoid communication with the cooperating teacher whenever possible. This would imply that particular attention be given to the successful efforts of the student teacher and that they should be built upon for further success.

Conferences may be held when special teachers have charge of the elementary classroom or during off-periods of secondary teachers. Frequently cooperating teachers and student teachers arrive early in order to have conferences before school or stay after school for this purpose. The latter is probably preferable since the conference is less likely to be interrupted and can be longer. The cooperating teacher must be willing to give his time for conferences or he should not accept a student teacher.

It is suggested that specific time limits also be placed on conferences so that participants may make personal plans accordingly. This also helps in keeping the conference in line with the particular aspects to be discussed rather than following tangential issues.

In anticipating a conference, both the cooperating teacher and the student teacher should be prepared. The cooperating teacher should have materials at hand to which he wishes to refer the student teacher as well as specific points outlined which are to be covered. The more specific he can make the conference, the more effective it will be. Student teachers should be prepared with specific questions concerning their teaching plans which have been developed, possible teaching materials, and an open mind.

The more successful the cooperating teacher is at conducting inductive conferences, the more the student teacher will grow as a result: Questions should be raised for the student teacher to answer which get to the points to be covered. His own self-analysis of his teaching is more beneficial to the student teacher than the cooperating teacher's analysis.

Early conferences should be concerned with providing help for the student teacher in becoming adjusted to his new role. Help can be given in planning early observations and in evaluating them to insure that the student teacher is learning from them. Special interests and weaknesses of the student teacher can be determined with help provided to capitalize on strengths and strengthen weaknesses detected. These early conferences also help considerably in providing opportunities for the two parties to get to know one another better.

It is difficult to itemize a list of topics which should be covered in conference with the student teacher since conferences should be personalized as much as possible. Areas that are often covered, however, are the following:

1. Personal adjustment to teaching
2. Evaluation of observations
3. Acquaintance with pupils' backgrounds
4. Motivation of learning
5. Meeting individual differences
6. The educational classroom environment
7. Records and reports
8. Using teaching materials (including audio-visual)
9. Professional ethics
10. Planning classroom work
11. Evaluating the teaching performance

There are often other areas of more personal concern which should be covered. Even such intimate problems as personal grooming and personality defects may pose areas which need to be discussed. Such problems are often difficult to deal with but must be resolved. This is better done during student teaching than later when the problem may result in the loss of a teaching position. It is suggested that, if possible, these problems be covered after a good working relationship has been established to avoid possible hostility being created early in the experience.

Once the student teacher has reached the point where he is assuming major teaching responsibilities, the focal point of most conferences will be in the area of developing plans and evaluating what has taken place. In no circumstances should the student teacher be permitted to teach unless he has developed plans to guide him. Since the cooperating teacher is responsible for the instruction in his classroom, he should desire to approve all plans prepared by the student teacher.

The term "conference" implies participation by two or more people. There should be as much active participation by the student teacher as by the cooperating teacher. The cooperating teacher who succeeds best is one who is able to get the student teacher to become an active member of the conference activity.

Trimmer listed the deficiencies of cooperating teachers in the judgment of student teachers who had completed the course. Most of these were areas reflecting poor conferences. In order of frequency of mention, these deficiencies were:

1. Lack of constructive criticism
2. No regular conferences
3. Never allowed control of the class
4. No suggestions as to methods and techniques
5. Freedom but no guidance
6. Lack of organization
7. Rigidity
8. Not frank in criticism
9. Poor attitude towards pupils
10. Inflexibility in teaching methods[1]

The lack of constructive criticism is one of the most frequently-mentioned complaints of student teachers. They desire much more than a pat on the back and a general "good job" comment. They feel that they are enrolled in student teaching for help and criticism and feel cheated when this is not forthcoming.

No discussion of conferences would be complete without mention of the necessity for three-way conferences including the college supervisor with the other parties involved. Such conferences do much to maintain common understandings and prevent conflicts from arising. As a consultant, the college supervisor should have much to offer to all phases of the student teaching experience. The conference offers the best avenue to take full advantage of the college supervisor's professional knowledge and past experiences in working with many student teachers.

[1] Russell L. Trimmer, "Student Teachers Talk Back," Journal of Teacher Education, December, 1960, p. 537.

Planning for successful teaching

No aspect of student teaching is more critical to the ultimate success of the student teacher than the planning which takes place as he assumes the active teaching role. True, even superior planning does not compensate for poor personality factors or for lack of subject matter knowledge, but it is necessary if the prospective teacher is to capitalize on his personality assets and organize his knowledge in such a way that he can be an effective teacher. Since it is assumed that the screening process has eliminated most of those who should not be in the classroom, the planning involved remains an important variable in promoting the student teacher's success.

During the initial stages of student teaching, the prospective teacher is very dependent upon the cooperating teacher, or at least should be. He takes his cues from the cooperating teacher as to materials to be used, ways of reaching the class, motivation, activities and procedures to be utilized, and methods of evaluating pupil progress. This is the time when considerable help in planning is necessary. Often cooperating teachers make more detailed teaching plans for themselves at this time than they would ordinarily make in the light of their teaching experience in order that the student teacher might have more security in learning how to plan. Many teachers have the early teaching assignments stem from their own plans, always making certain that the student teachers understand the "whys and wherefore" of what they are doing.

This early step of having the student teacher teach from the cooperating teacher's plans can be a distinct help to the student teacher. Such a procedure gives him the security he needs in his early classroom contacts; it gives him the benefit of plans formulated by an experienced teacher; and it results in successful teaching from the beginning which is a source of self-confidence for anyone. This does add a burden to the cooperating teacher in making and explaining such plans to the student teacher but might pay dividends later when the student teacher makes plans of his own.

The student teacher usually has had some experience in making lesson plans in his professional courses preceding student teaching, but effective planning can only be done in connection with actual teaching. The theoretical bases for planning, learned in various methods courses, provide necessary background; but planning for a specific group of learners followed by the actual use of the plan adds a new dimension to the experience.

Oftentimes in the very early days of the student teaching experience, the student teacher works with small groups of pupils. This may range from a reading group in an elementary class to a research committee in a secondary class. Even in such relatively simple aspects of teaching as these, there should be some planning or outlining of what is to be accomplished. The cooperating teacher can be of help in such assignments as these.

All plans developed by the student teacher should be approved by the cooperating teacher before they are put into operation. This serves not only to inform the teacher of what the class will be doing but also gives him an opportunity to suggest improvements or materials or to delete certain activities which are not appropriate. It also assures the teacher that the student teacher has adequately planned for his teaching assignment. The procedure of planning in advance for approval should be a standard procedure of the student teaching assignment throughout the semester or period of student teaching. If the cooperating teacher is interested in the welfare and progress of his pupils as he naturally should be, it behooves him to take an active part in the planning of the student teacher and in approving such plans, for this is a very important part of the learning experiences provided for his classroom pupils.

There are several reasons for insisting that student teachers develop competent teaching plans. Among them are:

1. Plans assure the cooperating teacher that the student teacher's efforts will be centered around the desired content area.
2. Plans provide the student teacher with a plan of action which has been approved by an experienced teacher who is familiar with the specific class involved.
3. Plans give the student teacher confidence and security.
4. Plans provide a checklist for the student teacher to make certain that all necessary materials are available when needed.
5. Plans give the university supervisor an outline of what the student teacher is doing in the classroom for his general information or as a guide for classroom visitation.

6. Plans assure a businesslike approach in the student teacher's actual instruction.
7. Plans help the student teacher begin a file of useful materials for later reference.
8. Plans aid in maintaining classroom control.

The last-mentioned reason for requiring careful planning by the student teacher was touched upon earlier. Years of experience in working with student teachers have convinced the writer that there is no better way of maintaining the proper decorum in the classroom than by having well-developed teaching plans which keep the pupils constructively busy and interested. When student teachers realize this, their plans take on a new perspective for them.

Although the cooperating teacher should provide much guidance in the beginning planning, the student teacher should be encouraged to use his own ideas and display as much initiative as possible as he becomes more proficient in the planning procedure. Student teachers learn much from experimenting and from trial and error. This can be done up to a point without the pupils' suffering from such approaches. It must be remembered that the student teacher must develop his own unique teaching skill which may or may not emulate the cooperating teacher. Plans must reflect this.

Following the early "helping" teaching assignments, the student teacher begins to approach the time when he will assume more and more of the teaching responsibility, involving more and more planning. As soon as the student teacher has reached the point where his teaching assumes so much time that short, incidental conferences will not provide the necessary planning, it is necessary that major emphasis on planning be given. The first lesson plans of the student teacher involving major teaching responsibilities, perhaps for the entire class period, should be jointly made. This means exactly what it says--joint planning. The cooperating teacher and the student teacher together can easily outline the necessary facets of the teaching plan for student teacher use. Actually, there are occasional cooperating teachers who plan jointly with the student teacher in developing lessons which the cooperating teacher himself uses as an intermediate step before the student teacher assumes the major teaching responsibility. This procedure has much to offer. The joint planning approach gives the student teacher careful guidance in first-hand planning. It might be said that teaching by demonstration in planning is as effective as in showing methods of conducting a class.

As soon as the student teacher has found himself and has the self-confidence desired, he can gradually assume more and more of the responsibility of planning his own teaching. All early plans, those jointly made and those made later by the student teacher alone, should be prepared in detail. It may be that before the student teaching experience is over, the student will be able to teach effectively from abbreviated plans, but this should not be encouraged too greatly. He still lacks experience; it is better to plan in too much detail than have plans not detailed enough.

During the student teaching experience, the college student needs to be aware of many kinds of plans. He needs to know the long-range plans of the teacher for the semester and year's work. He needs to know the fundamentals of unit planning for a long period of time and of daily lessons for day-by-day teaching. He must know the relationship of what he is teaching to the overall curriculum. The student teacher should get some actual experience in as many kinds of advanced planning as can be worked into his experience profitably.

If a unit plan is to be required of the student teacher, a definite unit or major content area should be determined early in the student teaching assignment along with the approximate time when the unit will be taught. The preparation of a unit should cover several weeks if the unit is to be well developed. Most experienced teachers need several weeks to plan a resource unit--the inexperienced student teacher needs every bit as much time if not more. This necessitates an early commitment to a specific unit of work. While plans are proceeding on the selected unit, the student teacher may continue with other teaching assignments on a daily basis.

Regardless of whether the teaching plan is a long range effort or a daily lesson, the basic ingredients are the same. The student teacher must know what he hopes to accomplish in his teaching, *i.e.*, the overall objectives or the aims of his teaching plan. While he must not lose sight of general objectives of the particular subject or course, he should focus his attention on the specific outcomes of his immediate teaching. He must then decide on how the outcomes can best be achieved by the pupils, taking into consideration the available materials, the ability of the pupils, the teaching methods which seem most appropriate, and the relationship of the content and aims to what has preceded the lesson and what will follow it. He must then plan his evaluation procedure to determine the extent to which his objectives have been reached.

Once the teaching plan has been made, the cooperating teacher must be alert to its proper use. Student teachers often go to either of two extremes in their teaching. The lesson plan is rigidly followed with little deviation permitted by some student teachers while others pay too little attention to what they have written down and permit the class discussion to wander far afield. Student teachers must learn that lesson plans are developed as guides for teaching and should be generally adhered to; however, they must also develop a sensitivity to the appropriateness of following tangents or related areas when the opportunity arises. This is not as simple a task as it may seem. Student teachers realize that they are not in complete charge of any class and that their work must fall within the permissible framework of the cooperating teacher's overall plans. This often prevents the student teacher's taking advantage of opportunities for enlarging upon a particular concept even if he realizes that the opportunity is present. The flexibility of lesson plans should be pointed out to him and impressed upon his mind.

There is another aspect of planning with student teachers which should probably be mentioned. There is more involved than merely planning with the student teacher, making suggestions, and watching him put the plan into effect. Prior to making further plans, the cooperating teacher and the student teacher should evaluate the last plans made with particular emphasis upon their effectiveness. Questions might be raised as to why particular activities were successful or why others were less satisfactory. The appropriateness of some materials or the effectiveness of others are often not discernible until they have been used with pupils. The concept of evaluating the lesson plans and the teaching as well as the evaluation of pupil progress should be a distinct part of the student teaching experience.

There is no one way in which all lesson plans should be prepared. The actual format is not as important as the content and procedures to be followed. Plans must be in such form, however, that there is sufficient clarity that the cooperating teacher and the student teacher can easily understand what is to be done. It goes without saying that the plan should be logically formulated so that the student teacher may move easily from one activity to another without taking time out to interpret what he has written in the plan.

ADDITIONAL REFERENCES

Allen, Arthur T. and Dorothy I. Seaberg, "Teachers-in-the-Becoming," *The Elementary School Journal*, 64:332-339, March, 1964.

Casey, John P. and Lois Lilly, "How Do Student Teachers Spend Their Time?" *Illinois Education*, 51:194, January, 1963.

Curtis, Dwight K. and Leonard O. Andrews, *Guiding Your Student Teacher*, New York: Prentice Hall, Inc., 1954.

Devor, John W., *The Experience of Student Teaching*, New York: The Macmillan Company, 1964, pp. 270-353.

Haines, Aleyne, *Guiding the Student Teaching Process in Elementary Education*, Chicago: Rand McNally Publishing Co., 1960.

Houston, W. Robert, Frank H. Blackington, III, and Horton C. Southworth, *Professional Growth Through Student Teaching*, Columbus, Ohio: Charles E. Merrill Books, Inc., 1965, pp. 156-212.

Murphy, Geraldine, "The Prospective Teacher as Observer," *The Journal of Teacher Education*, 13:150-156, June, 1962.

Telfer, Harold E. and William R. Sleeper, "The Student Teacher Conference: A Must!" *Peabody Journal of Education*, 41:169-172, November, 1963.

Chapter VII

The Evaluation of Student Teaching

If the prospective teacher is to improve in his personal and professional competencies, it is essential that proper evaluation of his growth be incorporated into the student teaching experience as a planned and integral part. Paramount to good evaluation is an awareness of the purposes of student teaching, an understanding of the student teaching personality, the ability to analyze the teaching process, and the willingness of all parties to participate in free and open discussion. If these components are present, evaluation cannot help but result in constructive and profitable ends.

Evaluation in student teaching means the mutual analysis of successes and failures and the identification of the causes of each with an eye toward the continual improvement of the student teacher in his teaching role. Only in this way can progress towards the goals of student teaching be made. In considering the evaluation of student teaching, one must look far beyond the usual marking or awarding of grades with which the student teacher is familiar in his other college courses and which usually constitutes his understanding of evaluation.

Principles of evaluation

Basic to proper evaluation in student teaching are several fundamental principles which must be used as frames of reference in planning the evaluative approach. These are generally accepted by those who work regularly with student teachers as leading to the most desirable results. These principles are:

1. Evaluation is cooperative and centered around self-evaluation
2. Evaluation is continuous
3. Evaluation is comprehensive
4. Evaluation is specific
5. Evaluation is individualized

Evaluation is cooperative and centered around self-evaluation. The word evaluation itself implies cooperative interaction as opposed to grading which implies imposed judgment. The student teacher must be as active in participating in evaluation as the cooperating teacher or college supervisor. The goal of all evaluation is to bring about desired behavioral change on the part of the student teacher. In order that persistent behavioral change may result, the student teacher must attain an understanding and an appreciation of the evaluative process in an active role. Only in this way can the student teacher develop a sensitivity as to what constitutes good teaching and become really aware of his own weaknesses and his strengths. One cannot overcome his shortcomings unless he first recognizes that they exist. After meeting the issue squarely, he can then develop plans for improvement.

Considerable skill is necessary on the part of the cooperating teacher if the proper climate is established wherein evaluation in this way can take place. Student teachers must feel secure to the point where they can accept suggestions without fear as well as raise questions without hesitation. Obviously, the proper climate is created by the cooperating teacher's doing much more than merely telling the student teacher what is wrong.

The inductive approach of leading the student teacher to recognize his own problems offers the best procedure. This requires tact and insight on the part of the classroom teacher or supervisor. The student teacher is often in a position where he senses that his teaching is not accomplishing the desired result, but he needs help in determining why he is having difficulty. Once the problem is identified and accepted, the next step of seeking improvement generally requires the cooperating teacher to make concrete suggestions or to offer alternative approaches for the student teacher to consider. If the student teacher can be led into discovering these alternatives for himself, the result will be even better.

Evaluation is continuous. Just as growth in teaching skill is a continuous process, so must evaluation keep pace in a continuing fashion. The student teacher comes in contact with various aspects of the teaching role from his first day in the student teaching assignment. As he participates in various teaching activities, he needs to evaluate the purposes, the procedures, and the overall performance of the particular teaching function involved. As he progresses to more complex teaching activities, this evaluation becomes more complex. If an evaluative climate is created from the initial experience, it becomes easier to understand the more complex evaluations of later teaching experience.

Continuous evaluation implies regular and periodic analyses in order that weaknesses may be identified for specific improvement and strengths isolated upon which the student teacher and cooperating teacher may build. Evaluation starts with the first meeting of cooperating teacher and student teacher, for at this time the impressions made and information solicited begin to lay the groundwork for the student teaching experience and subsequent evaluation. It should be made a part of every conference as well as a part of every individual analysis of teaching and planning.

By no means should the evaluation of student teaching resolve itself only into periodic check-ups or be left to the conclusion of the student teaching assignment for an intensive review of the experience and the student teacher's performance. If the student teacher is to profit from evaluation, it must be regular, consistent, and an integral part of the overall experience from the outset. If this is done, evaluation takes a positive approach; limiting it to a final overview makes evaluation take a negative slant.

Evaluation is comprehensive. Anything that the student teacher is assigned to do should have sufficient educational value that evaluation is involved. The teaching role is so complex today that one must look beyond the specific teaching act itself into the many complexities which make up the competent teacher. This involves working relationships, professional ethical behavior, understanding of young people, personality and professional zeal, as well as the knowledge of the subject matter which the student teacher possesses and the methods of transmitting knowledge to the pupils in his classes.

Far too often attention is given to the actual teaching process and its immediate facets while the many auxiliary duties of the student teacher go relatively unnoticed insofar as evaluation is concerned. This is easy to understand since the actual classroom involvement is the crux of good teaching; however, the many minor tasks in which the student teacher is involved need to be evaluated also. One cannot assume that the student teacher needs no help nor suggestions with respect to the relatively minor roles which he is called upon to perform. Evaluating such simple assignments as writing on the chalkboard, collecting papers, or distributing supplies and materials might result in improved legibility of handwriting, or a more orderly and economical procedure in classroom routines.

Evaluation is specific. One of the biggest weaknesses in the evaluation of student teaching, according to the student teachers themselves, is the lack of specific criticism and constructive suggestions for improvement. It is easy to deal in generalizations but student teachers need specific help. Generalizations often fall short of the mark and fail to make the necessary impression. For example, it is not enough to decide, even through cooperative means, that the student teacher needs to provide more motivation for his pupils. This must be accompanied by the cooperative agreement as to what specific steps might be tried to provide such motivation. It is not enough to decide that a test constructed by the student teacher is inadequate; it must be pointed out how it can be improved.

One common failing of cooperating teachers is to react to a particular teaching effort of the student teacher with an "everything is going fine" comment. This usually leaves the student teacher with a great deal of uncertainty for he knows that there is room for improvement. He wants specific criticism. The college student is enrolled in student teaching to learn and expects to make errors in the learning process. It is even worse for the cooperating teacher to make no comments about what the student teacher has done, for this is indeed most perplexing to the prospective teacher. If particular activities in which the student teacher participates are well done, he should be told of his success; if others are less successful, he should be made aware of them as well as the reasons for his lack of success.

There may be occasions when specific criticism must be pointedly made if the inductive process has not resulted in the student teacher's realization of a particular problem. These criticisms should not be avoided if the student teacher can profit from them. This is a part of the responsibility assumed by the cooperating teacher when he agrees to accept the student teacher.

Offering constructive criticism requires skill and abilities not commonly found. Criticism is easy to offer, but constructive criticism involves not only the careful analysis of what is wrong but also specific suggestions for correction. The degree to which the student teacher can accept and profit from suggestions varies as one might expect. Improvement resulting from cooperating teacher suggestions depends upon the way in which such suggestions are made.

Evaluation is individualized. If one accepts the premise that individual differences exist among student teachers, then it follows that the evaluation of the student teaching experience must be planned to fit into the situation as it exists. One must not expect all student teachers to progress at the same rate nor to reach the same level of competency in all aspects of the teaching role. Some student teachers may have problems which require more careful attention than others just as they may have some strengths which others lack. It is difficult to keep from comparing student teachers with others which the cooperating teacher has known, but an effort should be made to refrain from so doing if the evaluation is to be objective and individualized for the specific student teacher under consideration.

It is for this reason that the knowledge and understanding of the student teacher's personality has been stressed. Evaluation must be based on the individual characteristics and abilities of each student teacher.

It is important for the cooperating teacher to keep in mind that the student teacher is not an accomplished teacher but is in the classroom to learn how to teach. The student teaching performance must be evaluated with an eye toward starting with the student teacher where he is and looking for a steady, continuous growth.

Evaluative instruments

There are various techniques used in evaluating the progress of the student teacher. The best approach is through direct communication in carefully planned conferences directly related to the area of teaching under consideration. In such conferences many cooperating teachers and college supervisors utilize evaluation instruments. The popularity of check-lists, rating scales, or other such forms is probably due to the fact that they identify specific areas to be touched upon and present common elements for evaluation regardless of who is evaluating the student teacher. They also present the student teacher with specific criteria upon which he knows he will be evaluated. A printed form also provides a permanent record of the student teacher's competency which lends itself to inclusion in the placement credentials or permanent file of the student. Often such records are needed for recommendations in future years.

The best kind of evaluative instrument attempts to describe in behavioristic terms the kind of procedures used by teachers and their effectiveness as they perform the teaching role. They are often arranged in a continuum from least desirable traits to most desirable with the expectation that the student teacher will be evaluated at some descriptive point on the continuum. An alternative form lists a series of specific aspects of teaching with a rating symbol to be assigned which best describes the performance of the student teacher in each function. Following are specimen evaluation forms illustrating both types.

Regardless of format, most evaluative instruments usually cover three basic areas concerning the student teacher and his competency. Often one finds items relating to the student teacher as an individual, touching upon such areas as personality characteristics, health, grooming, ethical behavior, etc.; to his professional preparation and knowledge, including the knowledge of subject matter as well as general educational background; and to his actual teaching performance as demonstrated through the various student teaching activities.

Evaluative instruments may be used in various ways. They present an excellent way for student teacher self-evaluation. Many cooperating teachers and supervisors complete the forms during conferences with student teachers; others have the student teacher rate himself for comparison with the rating of the cooperating teacher. In this way attention is drawn to the areas which are not agreed upon and all parties know where particular attention needs to be given.

If evaluation is to be cooperative and center around self-evaluation, the best use of rating scales and check lists would be the cooperative, analytical application of the items on the scale in an open discussion between student teacher and the evaluator, either the cooperating teacher or the college supervisor. This eliminates misunderstanding and misinterpretation of criteria and of suggestions.

STUDENT TEACHER EVALUATION FORM
College of Education : The University of Texas

____________________ (Student Teacher)

____________________ (University Supervisor)

____________________ (Teaching Field)

____________________ (Semester of Student Teaching)

DIRECTIONS: Please place a check mark on the appropriate place on each scale which best describes the rating of the student in comparison with other student teachers you have supervised. Underscore any descriptive phrase which is particularly appropriate to the student teacher.

PERSONAL QUALIFICATIONS:

	1 2 3	4 5 6	7 8 9
Personal appearance	Poor taste in dress and grooming	Usually makes a good impression	Excellent appearance; always appropriately dressed
Physical health and vitality	Lacks vitality; has physical handicaps which interfere	Satisfactory; adequate energy and drive	Excellent health and vitality
Voice	Not easily understood; unpleasing quality; inadequate volume, poor tone; lacks fluency	Easily understood; adequate volume; tone inflection	Pleasing, excellent inflection; proper modulation, volume, articulation
Communication skills	Incorrect speech; ungrammatical; slangy; limited vocabulary; ineffective communication	Acceptable written and oral expression; adequate vocabulary; handwriting acceptable	Effective communication; skillful choice of vocabulary; clearly legible handwriting
Emotional stability	Moody; irritable; rigid; immature; insecure; unwilling to face reality	Well-balanced emotionally; has ups and downs but does not go to extremes	Emotionally secure; good sense of humor; faces problems realistically
Interpersonal relationships	Cold; hostile; critical; defensive	Moderately effective in social relationships	Warm; outgoing; kind; understanding; free from affectation
Dependability	Unpredictable; does not follow through	Can usually be relied upon	Always reliable and punctual
Initiative	Little resourcefulness; waits to be told, depends on others	Does what he is told; follows directions; moderately successful	Enthusiastic; does more than required; sees a job to be done and does it

PROFESSIONAL QUALIFICATIONS:

	1 2 3	4 5 6	7 8 9
Knowledge of professional education	Narrow and superficial knowledge of educational concepts and skills	Satisfactory knowledge of professional education	Thorough and workable knowledge of educational concepts and skills
Commitment to teaching	Little interest; just getting by; bored; sometimes negative	Moderate interest and enthusiasm	Very enthusiastic; eager; alert; professional-minded

	1 2 3	4 5 6	7 8 9
Attitude toward professional help	Resents suggestions; rationalizes; reluctant to change	Accepts suggestions; makes effort to adapt them to teaching	Seeks suggestions and evaluations; profits from them
Improvement in professional competence	Little or no improvement; getting nowhere	Average improvement; satisfactory growth	Considerable improvement; rapid growth
Understanding of educational purpose	Vague; limited; misconceptions; lack of direction	Some understanding; occasional inconsistency	Highly perceptive; based on pupil and societal needs; sound sense of direction
Acceptance by other professional persons	Rejected; isolated; creates hostility	Accepted by others	Attracts; sought after; leader

TEACHING EFFECTIVENESS:

	1 2 3	4 5 6	7 8 9
Planning	Lacking in organization; continuity, variety in procedure; fails to see goals clearly	Generally well-organized; some variety in procedure; usually well-timed; needs frequent help in planning	Consistent long-range and daily planning; appropriate and meaningful objectives; creative and flexible
Use of plans	Plans poorly executed; goals not clearly in mind	Achieves goals fairly well; lessons usually proceed as planned though somewhat rigid	Well-executed plans with appropriate adjustments; capitalizes on unexpected learning opportunities; achieves goals; wise use of time
Recognition and provision for individual and group differences	Makes little effort to know pupils; little provision for individual differences	Aware of special needs; occasionally makes special provision for differences and needs	Strives to know pupils; sensitive to differences and needs; varies content, materials, and activities to meet needs
Knowledge of subject matter	Inadequate knowledge of content; limited understanding of concepts	Average understanding of concepts; acceptable knowledge of the teaching field	Thorough understanding and extensive knowledge of the field; up-to-date
Motivation of learning	Fails to stimulate pupil interest	Generally achieves good pupil participation; pupils see some purpose in learning activities	Makes learning activities purposeful and stimulating
Selecting, preparing, and using instructional materials	Generally unsatisfactory choice and use of materials	Usually selects and prepares appropriate materials; fairly well used	Appropriate for purpose; advantageously used; good variety
Measurement and evaluation of learning	Unsatisfactory use of evaluative procedures; little relationship between evaluation and goals	Evaluative techniques are generally satisfactory; makes some use of evaluative findings in teaching	Appraises development in terms of well-conceived purposes; uses appropriate and varied procedures; evaluation used as a vital part of learning
Teacher-student relationships	Exceedingly lax in development of pupil self-control; poor handling of discipline problems; generally does not have respect of pupils	Fairly effective development of pupil self-control and cooperation; usually has pupil respect	Maintains democratic cooperative spirit; develops pupil self-control and responsibility; encourages pupil initiative; respects pupils and their ideas
Classroom management	Gives little or no attention to the learning environment; poor management	Satisfactory attention to routine factors; average effort to provide stimulating learning environment	Provides stimulating, attractive learning environment; manages routine well; makes adjustments for health and comfort

MIAMI UNIVERSITY EVALUATION OF STUDENT TEACHING ELEMENTARY FORM

Student__________ School and District__________ Trimester and Year__________

Grade and Subject__________ Cooperating Teacher__________ University Supervisor__________

DIRECTIONS: This form is designed to be used by the cooperating teacher, the university supervisor, and the student teacher, to evaluate achievement in teaching competency at mid-term and at other appropriate times. The university supervisor, in consultation with the cooperating teacher, has the responsibility for the final evaluation at the close of the trimester.

EXPLANATION OF THE TERMS:

Outstanding - Is a professional person with extraordinary promise. This performance is rarely seen in student teaching.

Strong - Is considerably better than average in teaching competence. Should do a superior job during the first year of teaching.

Acceptable - Is adequately prepared to begin teaching. Should do satisfactory work during the first year of teaching.

Weak - Will need considerable help and supervision during the first year of teaching.

	O	S	A	W
I. TEACHING COMPETENCIES				
A. PERSONAL AND PROFESSIONAL QUALITIES				
1. Shows physical vitality and enthusiasm				
2. Is always neat and well-groomed				
3. Has a pleasant and effectual teaching voice				
4. Exercises emotional control and poise				
5. Demonstrates interest in children and in teaching				
6. Takes initiative in assuming responsibility				
7. Carries out all tasks effectively and punctually				
8. Accepts and profits from constructive criticism				
9. Works cooperatively with others				
10. Is aware of the need for continued professional growth				
B. INSTRUCTIONAL COMPETENCIES				
1. Understands and applies the principles of child growth and development				
2. Assists pupils in developing habits of democratic living				
3. Has an adequate knowledge of content material				
4. Relates subject matter and activities to the interests and age and maturity levels of the children				
5. Writes effective plans				
6. Shows initiative and imagination in careful planning for all learning activities				
7. Demonstrates skill in the use of a variety of teaching techniques				
8. Selects a variety of appropriate teaching materials and has them available for immediate use				
9. Uses methods designed to reach and maintain the attention of all pupils				
10. Gives directions clearly				
11. Is flexible in adjusting plans as the need arises				
12. Utilizes questions which provide for group discussion and participation				
13. Develops effective processes of problem solving and critical thinking on the part of the pupils				
14. Develops a questioning attitude and intellectual curiosity in pupils				
15. Guides children in developing good work habits				
16. Evaluates in terms of individual differences				
17. Uses vocabulary suitable to the developmental level of pupils				
18. Uses spoken language correctly and effectively				
19. Writes legibly				
20. Spells correctly consistently				
II. GENERAL EFFECTIVENESS AS A TEACHER				

III. COMMENTS (Use other side)

INDIANA UNIVERSITY
School of Education
Final Evaluation of Student Teaching

Name of Student Teacher ______________________ Date ______________

CHARACTERISTICS AFFECTING TEACHING SUCCESS

Directions: Check the appropriate position on each scale. Underline strong points. Encircle weak points.

	Superior			Average				Inferior
1. CLASSROOM PERSONALITY Is mentally alert; has sense of humor; exercises self-control; has sparkle, drive and vitality; is poised and confident; is cheerful.								
2. PERSONAL APPEARANCE Exhibits good taste and neatness in dress; is clean; has no distracting mannerisms; is refined and cultured.								
3. SOCIAL QUALITIES Is friendly, understanding and helpful; is courteous and tactful; is interested in pupils; has ability to get along with others and understand their problems.								
4. LOYALTY AND COOPERATION Is willing and able to take suggestions and criticisms; cooperates with associates and supervisors; upholds school policies.								
5. HEALTH Has good general physical condition and mental health; able to carry normal load with energy in reserve; is free from trivial worries; has good posture.								
6. PROFESSIONAL ZEAL Is interested in teaching; takes steps toward self-improvement; is an enthusiastic worker; believes that teaching is worthwhile.								
7. GENERAL KNOWLEDGE AND INFORMATION Has a wide variety of interests and a broad understanding of the social scene.								
8. KNOWLEDGE OF SUBJECT MATTER IN TEACHING FIELDS Has an understanding and a working knowledge of content in teaching areas.								
9. ABILITY TO ORGANIZE MATERIALS FOR TEACHING PURPOSES Makes adequate plans for teaching; selects materials with due regard for individual differences; organizes materials effectively.								
10. ABILITY TO ORGANIZE LEARNING SITUATIONS Has general mastery of method; is able to create effective learning situations; obtains wide pupil participation; maintains proper balance between teacher-pupil activity; provides for individual differences.								
11. CLASS ACHIEVEMENT Achieves his objectives in the light of pupil abilities; selects appropriate appraisal techniques.								
12. CLASSROOM MANAGEMENT AND DISCIPLINE Is fair and just in dealing with pupils; secures good working conditions; understands pupils and their needs; is concerned for the physical welfare of pupils; has the interest and cooperation of pupils; develops social responsibility in pupils.								
13. VOICE AND SPEECH Is clear and distinct; has good inflection and modulation; is easy to understand; uses correct pronunciation; is free from irritating mannerisms.								
14. USE OF ORAL AND WRITTEN ENGLISH Has ability to present ideas simply and clearly; uses good English in and out of the classroom.								

IMPORTANT:
A written progress report and signature must appear on the back of this sheet

INDIANA UNIVERSITY SCHOOL OF EDUCATION
FINAL APPRAISAL OF STUDENT TEACHING

Name of Student____________________________________ Date__________________________.

THIS IS THE MOST IMPORTANT PART OF THE RATING OF THE STUDENT TEACHER.

The written appraisal to be entered below should be reasonably detailed, complete, and accurate. It should offer a fair appraisal of the over-all teaching effectiveness and potential of the student teacher. It should set out clearly his points of strength; and, if there be deficiencies, either inherent or remediable, these too should be mentioned. In general, the statement should be the kind that you would want to receive if you were a hiring official considering the student teacher as a candidate for a job in your school. This form will become a part of the student teacher's permanent record in the Bureau of Educational Placement.

Signed________________________________ Supervising Teacher in__________________________.

Evaluative forms also serve a useful purpose in orienting the college supervisor and the cooperating teacher toward the same ends so that the student teacher is not caught between two points of view. They promote understanding between the two supervisory positions as to the growth of the student teacher and provide the basis for suggestions from both for improvement.

Often profiles may be drawn from the scale used with student teachers. Care should be taken in attempting to make a profile of the various ratings since some of the items on the rating scale are often much more important than others and should be given more weight in attempting an overall description.

The check list type of evaluative instrument offers some possibilities in guiding the overall activities of the student teacher into the many facets of the teaching role. They often list many activities in which the student teacher may participate and suggest opportunities for learning which might be overlooked without the check list reminder.

Check lists, *per se*, offer few opportunities for evaluation; however, when used as a basis for conferences, they suggest many areas which need to be discussed and examined critically. They can focus attention upon activities in which student teacher participation has been limited and can aid in developing the comprehensive nature of the student teaching experience.

One of the problems in the use of the check list is the quantitative nature of such lists as opposed to the qualitative aspects of teaching. The quality of the student teacher's experiences is as important, if not more so, than the quantity of such experiences. One must not overlook this aspect of evaluation as he blithely checks off activities in which the student teacher has participated. A few check lists attempt to include the qualitative aspects of participation although this is difficult to do.

Grades and grading

The conventional student teaching program terminates in a letter grade awarded to the student teacher--therein creating one of the major problems of the student teaching course.

Many questions are raised by grading procedures. One can well understand the existence of the practice, for the awarding of grades is a time-established custom of higher education. One who is familiar with the fallibility of grades, however, might question its continuing existence as a part of the student teaching evaluative process.

Since the grade awarded and the credit earned become a part of the student teacher's college record, it would seem obvious that the official grade must be made a matter of record by the college supervisor who is the official college instructor charged with the experience of student teaching. In actual practice, the classroom cooperating teacher, who is often ostensibly declared to be an adjunct to the college staff but who is not usually officially recognized as such, is the one who knows the most about the student teacher's competency. It would seem a natural occurrence for the two supervisory persons to confer and agree as to the grade to be awarded to the student teacher involved.

Problems appear at this point. During the course of the student teaching assignment, the classroom teacher often identifies with the student teacher to the point where he feels that the success of the student teacher is analogous to his own success. Often, close friendships are formed and the relationships become even more complex. Many college supervisors say that nearly all classroom teachers indicate that their student teachers deserve an "A" grade.

Because of these complications, supervisors often do not talk with classroom teachers about grades specifically but try to restrict conferences to "evaluation" rather than "grading." If the cooperating teacher can look at the student teacher objectively and disassociate the close working relationships, the supervisor would in all probability be quite willing to take any recommendation of the teacher in determining the student's grade.

Above and beyond the problems involved in the grade to be awarded is the more basic issue of whether or not a grade *should* be given. Many excellent colleges have discontinued the practice of "grading" student teachers and record only a symbol indicating passing or failing. There seems to be a slight trend in this direction. Supplementing the recorded symbol is usually an evaluation form which attempts to describe the various aspects of the student teacher's proficiency.

The reasons stated for this change in practice are many but the essence of the arguments for the movement is the impossibility of narrowing down to a single letter grade the many facets of the complex teaching role. Student teachers have certain strengths, specific weaknesses, and differing personalities all of which affect the ultimate competency in teaching. To reduce these to a common denominator of a single grade is impractical and usually unfair to both student teacher and prospective employer. When one includes the extreme range of standards of many cooperating teachers and supervisors as well as the various kinds of classroom situations in which student teachers find themselves, it becomes even more complicated.

Many cooperating teachers and administrators who vociferously object to merit rating of teachers by claiming that exact determination of ability in the classroom is impossible apparently do not see the paradox of trying to grade student teachers as they are quite willing to accept this responsibility.

When grades are given in student teaching, it is not unusual to find the distribution of grades running quite high. Because of the fact that student teaching is usually a senior-level course, or the screening that takes place before admission, or the human factors involved, or the reluctance of administrators to employ students who make below a "B" in student teaching, or perhaps all of these, most grades in the course seem to be at the "A" or "B" level. This is probably a contributing factor in the movement toward elimination of the grade in student teaching.

In an institution in which grades are a part of the student teaching picture, an "A" grade should represent the best student teacher which the institution is capable of producing; a "B" student teacher should be one who does excellent work and is above average in potential; a "C" grade should represent the efforts of a student teacher who will do adequate work in the classroom. Any student teacher who falls below the "C" level should be looked at carefully to see whether or not he should be recommended for teacher certification.

The most important aspect of the entire problem is the self-evaluation which the student teacher employs to ascertain ways in which he can improve the contribution which he can make in the public school classroom.

Pupil rating

Questions are often raised concerning the feasibility of having pupils rate the student teacher and his performance. Indeed, there are many instances where such procedures are included as a part of the evaluative process. While some persons involved in student teaching feel that such procedures are valid and worthwhile for the student teacher, serious questions could be raised as to their inclusion in the evaluative picture.

Although classroom pupils are usually aware of the role of the student teacher, except for very young children, asking them to rate the performance of the student teacher eliminates one more aspect of respect which should exist between student teacher and pupil. If the student teacher is to be considered in the teaching role, he must be given the respect and authority which accompanies this role. Asking pupils to rate him tends to destroy this relationship.

One might question the maturity with which pupils can rate student teaching performance. If the analyzing of the teaching role is a complicated skill and involves a broad understanding of all the attendant complications, classroom pupils are woefully inadequate in undertaking such a significant job.

True, there are areas in which pupils can react if they are pointed up specifically enough. Pupils can react in terms of the student teacher's clarity of assignments, show of favoritism, speaking voice, and ability in providing explanations; however, a competent cooperating teacher should be able to provide guidance in these areas without resorting to pupil involvement. In dealing with more fundamental aspects of teaching such as planning work, evaluating pupils, selection of teaching materials, etc., the pupils are obviously inadequate in making judgments.

It would appear that pupil rating offers little of constructive value in promoting the growth of the student teacher.

ADDITIONAL REFERENCES

Byers, Loretta and Elizabeth Irish, *Success in Student Teaching*, Boston: D. C. Heath and Co., 1961, pp. 227-249.

Curtis, Dwight K. and Leonard O. Andrews, *Guiding Your Student Teacher*, New York: Prentice Hall, Inc., 1954, pp. 257-317.

Devor, John W., *The Experience of Student Teaching*, New York: The Macmillan Co., 1964, pp. 193-208.

Grim, Paul R., Editor, *The Evaluation of Student Teaching*, Association for Student Teaching, 28th Yearbook, 1949.

McCabe, George E., "Evaluative Atmosphere: Evil or Asset?" *The Journal of Teacher Education*, 12:262-270, September, 1961.

Merriman, Pearl and Gladys M. Fair, *Helping Student Teachers Through Evaluation*, Association for Student Teaching, Bulletin No. 2, 1953.

Rippey, Andrew D., Editor, *Evaluating Student Teaching*, Association for Student Teaching, 39th Yearbook, 1960.

Chapter VIII

The Internship

A recent development in teacher education which has received a great deal of attention is the inclusion of an internship in the teacher preparation program. The internship has developed as a result of two factors; namely, to provide a vehicle for granting teacher certification to graduates with liberal arts degrees and to improve the quality of the teacher education program. Either or both factors have usually been responsible for internship programs which have been inaugurated.

The first factor evolved as college graduates desired to attain teacher certification at a post-graduate level and often resulted not only in the attainment of the teaching credential but also the granting of a master's degree as evidenced in the many Master of Arts in Teaching or similar programs found scattered across the country. The second factor was involved as teacher education institutions, recognizing the importance of actual experience as demonstrated in conventional student teaching programs, sought to extend this experience into a longer on-the-job association with actual teaching.

Although occasional efforts of internships for teachers may be found as far back as sixty years ago, it has only been in the last decade that the internship has been considered as a serious alternative to the customary teacher education program and been extended into numerous programs.

The internship differs from the conventional student teaching program in several ways. The primary difference is the cash payment which the intern receives for his teaching responsibilities which is not usually found in the conventional student teaching program. Other differences include the greater teaching responsibility which is assumed by the intern, a different form of supervision, and often a longer teaching assignment.

In most internship programs, the teaching intern is given a full-time teaching assignment in which he has the same responsibility as any duly-appointed teacher. For this work he is given a salary, usually somewhat less than that of a beginning certified teacher in the district in which he is working. This appointment, of course, usually involves a temporary teaching certificate or, in some cases, a special internship certificate to meet the legal requirements of teacher employment.

Supervisory responsibilities in internship programs vary. In many cases a college supervisor is involved in much the same way as in conventional student teaching programs. The primary difference comes about in the type of supervision provided by the public schools. In some cases the principal of the building in which the intern is employed assumes supervisory responsibility as he would any other beginning teacher, although he often devotes more time to the intern than he would give to a fully-certified teacher. In other situations, specific teachers are designated to oversee the work of the intern.

It is essential that some form of supervision be provided. If the internship is to be a learning experience for the prospective teacher, there must be guidance and evaluation of the teaching process. If it is not to be a learning experience, other than trial-and-error, there is little justification for the inclusion of the internship in any teacher education program.

One promising pattern which is found in a few cities provides for the employment of four or five interns who are given teaching assignments at a reduced salary from that of beginning teachers. With the difference in pay accumulated from the several interns, one experienced teacher is released from part or all of his teaching duties to serve as a supervisor for the group of interns. This teacher is then able to devote most or all of his time and energies to helping the intern in much the same manner as a cooperating teacher might help a student teacher. This assures close supervision which is sometimes lacking when no specific arrangements have been made.

The length of time in teaching also varies in internship programs. Many include a full year's teaching experience while others involve only one semester. The full year program is often easier to administer and is probably preferred by public school administrators. Semester-long internships usually involve matching interns whereby a new intern replaces one who is completing his experience at mid-year.

The newness of the internship concept has prevented any specific patterns from emerging as typical. Many programs include some professional course work in the summer preceding the internship with other courses being taken the summer following in order that a year's work may be included. This is particularly pertinent if a master's degree is involved in the program. Others include some professional work which is taken during the time of internship or in the semester following the teaching assignment. It would seem that, if possible, accompanying courses should not be taken during the time of actual teaching since the intern should be able to devote all his time and talents to his teaching responsibilities.

There can be no doubt, however, that some basic professional courses should be taken prior to the classroom assignment of the intern teacher. The internship involves the same necessity for knowledge of educational psychology and methods of teaching as conventional student teaching programs require. The sequence of the program should be carefully planned to insure the college student that he will be as ready for his internship experience as possible with those courses left to be taken following the internship which are content oriented and synthesizing professional courses which provide good culminating experiences.

Sleeper identified six characteristics of internships as reflected in college descriptions of several programs:

1. The internship has become the focal point in teacher preparing programs.
2. The emphasis on internship programs is one reason for the addition of fifth and sixth years to professional preparation.
3. There are experimental programs where the placement of the internship within the four or five year sequence is being examined.
4. Public schools are paying the intern in a number of programs.
5. The supervision in student teaching has been generally a one to one relationship, in some programs it will now be one to five or more.
6. A number of schools are providing a liberal arts program as a prerequisite to internship in the fifth or sixth year.[1]

[1] William R. Sleeper, "The Internship," Teacher Education and the Public Schools, 40th Yearbook, The Association for Student Teaching, 1961, pp. 71-72.

Most authorities prefer to have the internship preceded by a period of student teaching, if possible. Since the teaching responsibilities of the intern are great, it is thought that a brief acquaintance with teaching in the carefully guided and structured student teaching framework should enable the intern to begin his work at a greater level of competency than he would otherwise. This point of view is stressed by Boyan who said:

> ...The question is not whether a lengthier and more intensive internship is superior to conventional student-teaching experience in preparing the teacher, it is rather a question of the cost to the education of boys and girls with whom the intern works in the first few months on the job. Few observers raise questions about the effectiveness of interns as teachers in a postinternship year as compared to the effectiveness of conventionally prepared teachers in the first year of salaried experience, but some do question whether the intern is as effective a teacher during the early part of his first assignment as is the teacher who has completed a student teaching experience.[2]

This concept of pre-internship student teaching has led to some interesting efforts in providing variations of the usual student teaching experience.

In the Harvard Master of Arts in Teaching program, an intensive teaching experience is provided during summer school in which small groups of interns are given opportunities to teach in a special summer school program under the eye of a carefully selected classroom teacher, followed by a critique involving the fellow interns and the classroom teacher. Another interesting development is the micro-teaching experience developed at Stanford. In this program a simulated classroom situation is created involving a few pupils wherein the prospective teachers are exposed to specific teaching situations for a brief period of time. The teaching period is video-taped for later evaluation and self-study. Both pupils and supervising teacher evaluate the teaching performance.

[2] Norman J. Boyan, "The Intern Team as a Vehicle for Teacher Education," The Journal of Teacher Education, March, 1965, p. 22.

Central Michigan University has an internship program in which much interest has been shown and which has apparently been quite successful. One aspect of this program is the inclusion of three levels of internship assignments. During the junior year of college, the college student is assigned for a semester to a public school as a *teacher assistant*. The following year includes a second assignment for a semester as a *teacher extern* (an interesting title) with a final and third assignment during a fifth year of college as a *teacher intern*. Interesting aspects of this program are the alternate semesters of college work and public school assignments for a three year period of time, gradual increasing responsibilities for the prospective teacher at each level of assignment, and gradual increasing pay provided for the teacher commensurate with his increasing responsibilities.[3]

This program has a built-in pre-internship laboratory experience by spreading the teaching responsibilities over the three years. The only disadvantage one might find in the program is the possible added cost to the public schools with a possible disadvantage to the college student of needing five years to complete his college degree.

The advantages of the internship concept are several. When included in a professional program as a fifth year of preparation in either a five-year undergraduate program or as a fifth year of graduate work, the college student is somewhat more mature during his teaching than those usually enrolled in student teaching. He also brings to his first responsible teaching assignment a somewhat better background academically. By taking his professional courses in a framework blocked around the internship itself, he might be able to integrate theory and practice somewhat easier. At the same time, the college student is able to earn some income while still working toward his certificate. If the master's degree is involved, he begins his first year of teaching as a fully-certified teacher at a higher salary than he would on a conventional program in most cases. The biggest advantage of all, however, is the longer and more responsible teaching experience involved providing, of course, that there is frequent and suitable supervision of the teaching activities.

[3] Sleeper, op, cit., pp. 72-74.

One would be hard-pressed to find any disadvantages in well-structured and well-operated internship programs. If the proper supervision is not provided or if some type of teaching laboratory experience does not precede the internship, disadvantages could be identified. These, however, pertain to the quality of individual programs not to the concept of internship itself.

It would appear that selection procedures of prospective interns should be carefully refined and followed; incompetent interns can do far more damage to young minds than incompetent student teachers. The kind of person who can assume the responsibilities often required of interns is probably superior to those who can follow the conventional teacher education program with respect to self-confidence, knowledge of his subject matter, and adaptability.

It must also be emphasized that the college still bears the responsibility for supervision in the internship just as in student teaching. For a fully-developed quality program, the internship remains a cooperative endeavor for the college and the public school.

Although the internship concept has not spread in practice as rapidly as such other student teaching practices as full-time student teaching or off-campus assignments, it is generally considered as having a great potential for improving teacher education. The greatest limiting factors to its wider acceptance are apparently the added year of study which is involved in nearly all such programs and the slightly added cost to the public schools. It appears quite probable that as supply and demand of teachers become more equitable and with possible resultant increase in standards, the internship could easily become the conventional teacher education program of tomorrow. When and if the day arrives, the public schools will then become, through deliberate and overt action, the full partner in teacher education which many educators desire today.

ADDITIONAL REFERENCES

Boyan, Norman J., "The Intern Team as a Vehicle for Teacher Education," *The Journal of Teacher Education*, 16:17-24, March, 1965.

Fowlkes, John Guy, and Dean W. O'Brien, "The Teacher Internship--University of Wisconsin," *The High School Journal*, 47:132-137, December, 1963.

Haberman, Martin, "Intern Concept in Teacher Education," *Wisconsin Journal of Education*, 96:12-14, January, 1964.

Shaplin, Judson T. and Arthur G. Powell, "A Comparison of Internship Programs," *The Journal of Teacher Education*, 15:175-183, June, 1964.

Sleeper, William R., "The Internship," *Teacher Education and the Public Schools*, 40th Yearbook, The Association for Student Teaching, 1961, pp. 71-74.

Ward, William T., "Developing the Internship Concept in Oregon," *The Journal of Teacher Education*, 15:252-261, September, 1964.

White, Kenneth E., "A Plan for Student Interns in Teaching Positions," *The American School Board Journal*, 145:9-10, April, 1963.

Chapter IX

Descriptive Programs

Among the many teacher education institutions, one may find a wide variety of student teaching patterns and programs. In some respects this variety of programs represents a strength of teacher education in that no stereotype has developed which could eliminate experimentation and change with the possible result of static and dormant approaches. So long as there is variety, institutions tend to evaluate their own programs continuously and try to profit from the experiences of others as well, resulting in healthy growing programs of student teaching.

True, the variety of patterns sometimes results in confusion in the minds of public school teachers and administrators, particularly if several institutions with widely diverging patterns cooperate with the same school district. Reasonable approaches, however, can bring order out of such confusion to the net profit of all concerned.

Indicative of the variety which may be found are the following descriptions of actual programs. These descriptions were submitted by the institutions involved and reflect different approaches to the student teaching experience.

Indiana University[1]

Indiana University has two distinct programs of student teaching, one for elementary and one for secondary student teachers. Each program has a Director of Student Teaching.

At Indiana University elementary education majors are required to take 15 semester hours of student teaching during either the first or second semester of the senior year. In this program the student assumes partial or total responsibility for teaching one class in an elementary school selected by

[1] Contributed by V. E. Schooler, Director of Student Teaching in Secondary Schools, Indiana University, Bloomington.

the School of Education. A student who wishes a kindergarten or special education certificate must do approximately half of his work in student teaching in a kindergarten or special education classroom.

The program of student teaching in secondary schools is an off-campus, full-day assignment for a period of approximately eight weeks. Six semester hours of credit is the minimum for certification and eight hours of credit are usually earned at Indiana University. Regardless of the amount of credit the student expects to earn in student teaching, he must be in attendance in the assignment for the full eight week period.

Student teachers are placed in classrooms throughout the state with most students assigned in areas of concentration or centers. Approximately eight of these off-campus centers are utilized. The supervision of student teachers from the university is provided by area coordinators who are faculty members of the School of Education and a few experienced doctoral candidates who are interested in the student teaching program. Periodic seminars are held for student teachers. Indiana University is moving toward the employment of a full-time supervisory staff with full-time resident supervisors in the various centers.

The area coordinator (college supervisor) is a liaison person between the public school and the university. He is charged with the supervision of student teachers within a designated geographical area. Among his duties are the following:

1. To establish and maintain good relationships with the Board of Education, through the superintendent, by providing essential information about teacher education and student teaching in particular.
2. To help with the development of understanding the philosophy of teacher education as it operates within the framework of the public schools.
3. To assist principals in locating excellent and potentially effective supervising teachers.
4. To build good rapport with supervising teachers by holding conferences, providing materials, and giving help in the orientation and guidance of the student teacher.
5. To smooth the way for the student teacher and to set the stage for a high quality student teaching experience.

This includes directing the improvement of skills in teaching and in providing guidance in personal problems involved in the student teaching experience.

No letter grades, as such, are awarded upon the completion of the student teaching experience. The final efforts of the student teacher are reported as "S" for satisfactory or "F" for unsatisfactory. This mark is accompanied by a final evaluation form and recommendation.

Kent State University[2]

Student teaching at Kent State University is a full-time, off-campus program for one quarter of approximately eleven weeks. Students are eligible for student teaching as third quarter juniors and are counseled not to wait until the final quarter of their senior year. The elementary and secondary programs are similar except that the secondary students have a concurrent three-credit-hour course which meets every week on campus. In some curricula the assignment is split between two levels or areas, *i.e.*, primary-kindergarten, deaf-hearing, slow learning-average class. Twelve quarter hours credit are earned in student teaching which is offered each quarter of the academic year with a special program offered in summer school as described later.

The 1200 student teachers in this program during the academic year are supervised by seven full-time secondary and seven full-time elementary professors augmented by specialists in vocational home economics, men and women's physical education, kindergarten, and various special education fields. Over 80 per cent of the student teachers are assigned within forty miles of the campus, an area which includes the large urban complexes of Clevelend, Akron, Canton, and Youngstown.

Classroom supervising teachers are chosen by designated public school administrators using the requirements of the State of Ohio: three years of experience and a master's degree required for secondary levels and a bachelor's degree for elementary levels. In addition new supervising teachers must

[2] Contributed by Robert T. Pfeiffer, Director of Student Teaching, Kent State University, Kent, Ohio.

indicate a willingness to serve in this capacity. In a continuing relationship, Kent State University encourages repeated utilization of classroom teachers who demonstrate high level competency as supervising teachers. These teachers work with one student teacher at a time and are given a stipend of $70 per assignment.

Students applying for student teaching are given two choices of school systems. If for any reason a choice is inappropriate (German isn't offered in that system, for example), the problem is resolved at the time of application. These prospective student teachers must arrange and provide for their own transportation and housing during student teaching.

This organization, which avoids concentrating student teachers in a few school systems, necessitates cooperating with approximately 100 different school districts. Although this procedure has certain disadvantages, it has proven most defensible for a state-supported university in a heavily populated area. By stressing the selection of the supervising teacher rather than the district, a high premium is placed on the ability of the individual teacher.

Considerable emphasis is placed on the first visits by the college supervisor to inexperienced supervising teachers. The efforts of the college supervisor are supplemented by a handbook which includes suggestions selected to aid the classroom supervising teachers. A graduate class in supervision of student teaching is offered on campus and in the academic centers of the university.

In the first five-week summer session, student teaching is offered for three credit hours. Enrollment in this program is limited to individuals with three years of teaching experience. This opportunity allows the teacher employed without student teaching to meet the graduation requirement of student teaching without resigning his job and guarantees his entering the profession with some continuous supervision of his classroom performance. Opportunities in the summer program do not exist in all secondary fields. The campus laboratory school is used for student teaching in the summer program but at no other time.

Recently the entire college supervisory staff participated in an in-service program in which they learned Flanders Interaction Analysis. This endeavor was part of an attempt to sharpen supervisory techniques and insights and to go beyond casual and routine procedures. It is hoped that continued inspection of the means of analyzing teaching will put depth into the supervisory program.

St. Mary's University[3]

St. Mary's University, a church-supported liberal arts institution, maintains a relatively small teacher education program which prepares teachers for secondary schools only. During the current year approximately 75 student teachers will participate in the program. The university has been a co-educational institution for the past three years; prior to that its enrollment was restricted to men only.

The student teaching program involves a half-day assignment for a semester, taken during the senior year. Student teachers are required to spend a minimum of 180 clock hours in their assignments, at least 60 hours of which are to be spent in observation and allied activities with at least 120 clock hours involved in actual teaching experiences.

Student teaching assignments are made in the city of San Antonio and in three suburban school districts near the city. Placements in San Antonio are made through the public school supervisory staff and building principals while those in the suburban school districts are made directly with the principal of the secondary school building in which the student teachers have requested assignment.

All supervision falls in the general supervision pattern with faculty from the Department of Education assuming partial supervisory loads along with other teaching duties. Supervisors hold weekly individual conferences with student teachers for evaluation and planning. Eight seminars are held for groups of student teachers during the student teaching semester, coming more frequently during the initial stages of student teaching and spread out over slightly longer periods of time during the latter part of the student teaching assignment.

Classroom teachers are given no cash compensation for their services but cooperate in the program voluntarily as a

[3] Contributed by Miss Patricia Graham, Supervisor of Student Teaching, St. Mary's University, San Antonio, Texas.

professional contribution. This high level of cooperation as well as that of the public school administration staff has been a significant contribution to the quality of the student teaching program.

In a setting such as this the success of the teacher education program as well as student teaching is highly dependent upon the relationships existing between the Department of Education and other divisions of the university. The excellence of this relationship has also had a meritorious effect on the overall program.

The University of Texas

Two alternative programs of student teaching exist at The University of Texas. One, which includes the greater number of student teachers, consists of a half-day of student teaching for a semester for secondary student teachers with elementary student teachers following the same pattern with the addition of one full day each week. The second program, which operates in an off-campus center in San Antonio, provides for full-time student teaching for a half-semester.

The greatest strength of the student teaching program lies in the campus supervision which is provided and the excellent relationships which exist with the public schools. Specialized supervision is employed at the secondary level with all supervision provided by academic specialists in the College of Education. Supervisory loads are held at 18 student teachers for both elementary and secondary supervisors with no additional teaching responsibilities for the semester. This load and the fact that most student teachers are concentrated in either Austin or San Antonio results in close and frequent supervision. Supervisors visit student teachers weekly and hold weekly conferences and seminars.

Supervision is provided by faculty from the College of Education, selected doctoral students, and "rotating" teachers from the Austin Public Schools. The rotating teacher concept, which is somewhat unique, involves several teachers, four at the present time, who are given a year's leave of absence from the public schools and are employed by the university as supervisors of student teachers. These teachers are selected by the university from those nominated by the public school supervisory staff. All have master's degrees and have worked successfully with student teachers in the classroom.

Both rotating teachers and doctoral students enroll in a seminar in the supervision of student teaching taught by the Director of Student Teaching during the time in which they work with student teachers. This course coordinates their work with student teachers and provides them with insight and assistance in performing their supervisory duties.

Student teachers in selected areas such as physical education, home economics, art, music, and related fields are supervised by specialists from the department concerned who hold joint appointments in the College of Education. All have deep-seated interest in teacher education and have public school teaching experience.

Considerable emphasis is placed on research aspects of teacher education. At present, selected student teachers are involved in research projects in preparing teachers for working with culturally deprived children, in team teaching non-graded elementary schools and in studies in mental health for teachers and improvement of teacher personality.

Close relationships exist between the College of Education and the public schools, even to the point of securing judgments from the public school officials involved in the administration of student teaching when prospective faculty are employed who will be involved in the supervision of student teachers. All major policy change is the result of mutual study and approval.

At the present time, classroom cooperating teachers receive no cash compensation for their services in student teaching supervision. The university does provide consultant services to the Austin schools free of charge and furnishes a university-owned building to house a junior high school operated by the public schools. The public school teachers assume their roles as cooperating teachers as a professional obligation and are encouraged in this attitude by the public school administration.

The University of Tennessee[4]

The student teaching program at the University of Tennessee utilizes carefully selected centers located from twenty-five to one hundred miles from the campus. One staff member and about twenty students are assigned to each center, both coordinator and students devoting full time during the quarter to this experience. Each student teacher earns fifteen quarter hours college credit for the quarter's work.

Both elementary and secondary-level student teachers are included in each center. Students are advised to enroll in the program in the middle quarter of their senior year, thus allowing one quarter on the campus following student teaching. This permits careful evaluation and opportunity for remedial work.

Immediately after arriving in the community, student teachers begin the process of becoming more thoroughly acquainted with the school, the community and the children. While in the center they devote the full school day, five days each week and often the weekends, to the student teaching activities. They begin classroom observation and limited participation on the second day after arrival, and this leads to confirmation of specific teaching assignments and to responsible teaching as quickly as each student is ready.

When responsible teaching is actually begun, each secondary student teacher teaches from two to four classes daily (usually three), and the remainder of the school day is devoted to such assignments as the tri-weekly seminar, the school activities program, and further observation and participation in a variety of school activities. The elementary student teacher usually assumes full responsibility each day for one large block of time (three to four hours) in the class of his supervising teacher, and a shorter period is frequently devoted to some special teaching experience with a different grade level. At some time during the latter portion of the quarter it is expected that each student teacher will assume for a few days the complete teaching responsibilities of his supervising teacher.

[4] Contributed by E. S. Christenbury, Director of Student Teaching, The University of Tennessee.

In addition to the supervisory work of the coordinator, the subject area specialists in the College of Education are available to assist any student needing help. Some staff members of the Liberal Arts College have also made themselves available for consultant services to the coordinator and student teachers.

The tri-weekly seminar held in each center has been found by the coordinators to be most valuable in helping raise the horizon of the student teacher above the single teaching area or the individual classroom experience. This provides students an excellent opportunity to intellectualize their day by day experiences.

The classroom supervising teachers are selected by school principals and university coordinators. They are sometimes assisted in this selection by the subject area specialists at the university and the supervisors in the centers. A minimum of three years of experience, a master's degree and a genuine interest in working with student teachers are desired standards.

A very close working relationship is maintained between student teaching centers and the university. Supervising teachers and administrators are invited to the campus from time to time to evaluate the student teaching program. Occasionally, the university invites supervising teachers to spend the day at the university while the student teachers teach their classes. A special class for supervisors and directors of student teaching has been offered in some of the centers, on the campus, and as a workshop in the summer program.

The university pays the center $25.00 for each student teacher assigned full-time for the quarter. While the university exercises no control over what happens to this money, school administrators are advised to enlist the aid of teachers in determining the disposition of it. They often spend the money for something from which all teachers profit. This year an effort is being made to include the names of all supervising teachers in the staff section of the university catalogue.

A pre-student teaching seminar held weekly the quarter prior to student teaching has proved helpful. Through this seminar the students get to know their coordinators and the members of their group. They visit the student teaching centers, arrange for their housing and help their coordinators determine their appropriate teaching assignments. The policy of bringing to the campus representatives of groups in the process of doing their student teaching to talk with those going to the centers the next quarter has made a beneficial contribution to this seminar.

The university coordinators of student teaching, by virtue of the fact that they are in the school system almost continuously, have been most helpful in providing the essential orientation for the supervising teachers for their work with student teachers. The Student Teacher Manual developed especially for the supervising teachers and student teachers also makes a contribution to the orientation process.

Next year a special program will be developed for the preparation of selected classroom teachers who hope to become certified supervising teachers. Efforts will be made to secure scholarships to make it possible for these teachers to take advantage of the program. A doctoral program for the preparation of college supervisors and directors of student teaching is also being developed at the present time. Special scholarships will be sought to be awarded to promising teachers who are interested in the college side of student teaching administration and supervision.

Summary

One can see from these brief descriptions some common elements as well as some diversity. The importance of human relationships which exist and the necessity of cooperation between public schools and colleges are readily evident.

Both general and specialized college supervision may be found represented in the programs as well as differing lengths of student teaching assignments. Different plans of compensation for cooperating teachers are also included.

It should not be inferred that these illustrations represent the total variety which might be found in other institutions. There are many other patterns of programs which could be identified which differ from these considerably. They do, however, show the range which a random sample of student teaching programs reveals.

ADDITIONAL REFERENCES

Aden, Robert C., "An Experiment in Training Social Studies Teachers at North Texas State University, Denton," *Peabody Journal of Education*, 39:341-345, May, 1962.

Aldrich, Frederic D., "Preparing for Professional Teaching," *Educational Administration and Supervision*, 45:267-270, September, 1959.

Braun, Gertrude, "Cooperating Teacher Education Program," *Teacher Education Quarterly*, 17:15-18, Fall, 1959.

Nelson, Horace, "A Survey of Student Teaching Practices in Eight Southeastern States," *The Journal of Teacher Education*, 14:188-193, June, 1963.

Westfall, Byron L., "Student Teaching Programs in Certain School Systems of The North Central Association Area," *The North Central Association Quarterly*, 37:237-245, Winter, 1963.

Wilhelms, Fred T., "The San Francisco State College Teacher Education Project," *The Journal of Teacher Education*, 12:209-215, June, 1961.

Woodruff, Asahel D., *Student Teaching Today*, Study Series No. 5, Washington, D. C.: The American Association of Colleges for Teacher Education, 1960, pp. 30-38.

Chapter X

Issues and Trends

While student teaching continues to function, apparently successfully, there are issues which have not been fully resolved with respect to the operation of student teaching programs. Some of these are basic to the fulfillment of student teaching objectives while others are less significant. There are also some movements which indicate the direction which possibly may be followed in resolving these problems. Among the issues and trends which may be identified are the following:

1. *The role of the public school in teacher education.* Although expected to provide most of the elements of a successful student teaching experience, the public school has not been merged completely as a full partner in the teacher education enterprise. Ostensibly, the partnership exists; however, the college continues to decide the pattern of student teaching, the requirements for admission to the course, the qualifications for cooperating teachers, and reserves the assignment of grades in many instances. While few persons would have the college abdicate all of these responsibilities, the possibilities of public schools becoming more actively involved in the planning of student teaching policy might be desirable. A trend may be noted with respect to this issue; namely, the gradual inclusion of the public schools in more and more aspects of the student teaching experience. The cooperative supervisory arrangements used in some institutions, internship programs, and the interest manifested by such groups as the Commission on Teacher Education and Professional Standards of the National Education Association in this area are indicative of the trend.

2. *Qualifications of the cooperating teacher.* As the public schools assume more and more of the responsibility for student teaching and the cooperating teacher becomes increasingly more important, more attention is given to the criteria for the selection of cooperating teachers. The question of possible state certification for such roles is often raised. This has been applied with varying degrees of success in some

states. The lack of success in many instances is probably due to the lack of prestige and financial incentive provided teachers to secure such certification. Without these motivational factors encouraging certification as cooperating teachers, teachers are reluctant to become involved.

The Association for Student Teaching has shown increasing interest in this area with special commissions and committees actively involved in determining criteria for selection and recognition procedures for superior accomplishment in the field of working with student teachers.

The lack of agreement between colleges and public schools on what constitutes a good teacher needs to be resolved with agreement on ways of preparing competent cooperating teachers. Accompanying this issue is a trend toward teacher-education institutions providing more in-service education for teachers working in student teaching programs. As certification for cooperating teachers gains in scope and requirements are refined, colleges will undoubtedly become more and more involved in this area.

3. *Providing compensation for the supervisory job* The recent movement from cash compensation for cooperating teachers towards the assuming of the job as a professional obligation has not resolved the monetary problem. While dedicated teachers may undertake the supervisory role willingly enough without compensation, the lack of payment keeps the job in a charity relationship with colleges. Colleges, as a result, are often placed in an awkward situation with respect to the supervisory program and are often reluctant to require certain expectations of cooperating teachers. The recent interest in involving the state or possibly the federal government in the compensation picture portends things which may come. Stirrings of interest may be noted in the literature and in professional meetings. While it is not yet a trend, there are indications that the movement may become more significant within a few years.

4. *The student teaching pattern.* No clear-cut validated type of program of student teaching has yet been developed which clearly demonstrates specific patterns as superior to others. The variety of student teaching programs, while desirable in some respects, generally results in confusion in the public schools and lack of unity when institutions attempt to secure a united front in legislative or professional areas.

It is obvious that the minimal programs of some institutions provide far less competency than the more intensive student teaching programs of others. There is a trend toward making the experience as nearly like the first teaching position as possible. Full-time student teaching, semester-long programs, and the internship indicate the direction currently followed.

5. *The role of the college supervisor.* The professional status of the college student teaching supervisor has not yet become fully recognized to the extent its importance warrants. Often a job to be avoided by college professors, it survived the stage of being passed around to whoever had time available on his teaching load. Finally, the importance of the job has begun to assert itself, and it has begun to be recognized as a fully professional job in itself. Largely supported by accreditation associations, the supervisory position has reached the point where loads are becoming more reasonable, prestige is slightly greater, and the job is becoming more appealing to the faculty of teacher-education institutions. Cooperative arrangements with public schools appear to indicate an additional desirable aspect of the supervisory role.

6. *The legal status of the student teacher.* The lack of common law decisions in the absence of statutory provisions for student teaching has created a questionable status with respect to the legality of student teachers' assuming teaching responsibilities and the ensuing liability involved. More concern is being evidenced toward this problem and slowly states are beginning to solve the problem by taking appropriate legislative action to permit student teaching and to define its scope. As states participate more in financial aspects of student teaching and require state certification for cooperating teachers, the legal status of the student teacher will clarify itself.

7. *The evaluation of student teaching.* The realization that letter grades fail to provide prospective employers with sufficient information about the prospective teacher is slowly bringing about a change in evaluative concepts. Many academicians and college registrars still have to be convinced; however, there is some indication that letter grades for student teachers may eventually be replaced by more comprehensive evaluative instruments and procedures. This will necessitate the refinement of evaluative instruments and a re-education of personnel directors who employ the products of the student teaching program. Experimentation with the use of video-tape,

tape recorders, and sound film in analyzing the teaching performance indicates the newer approaches to student teacher evaluation. These, coupled with various research projects attempting to analyze the teaching act, could easily result in a much more comprehensive evaluative procedure in the near future.

8. *Professional laboratory experiences.* For many years, educators have desired more laboratory experiences and more participation in classrooms during the pre-service education of teachers. At present there is a decided movement toward incorporating more such experiences in professional courses. If a trend were to be identified, this would be it. The limitations of facilities for such experiences and the increasing number of teachers to be educated provide difficulties in attaining the desirable level of such experiences, however. There is considerable interest in the utilization of vicarious laboratory experiences in place of actual participation and observation. Several colleges are experimenting with film clips, closed-circuit television, and mass demonstration lessons in place of individual involvement in different situations. At least one experimental study indicated that such a program results in as competent development of concepts of teaching as direct observation if not better.[1] In predicting future developments in the area of professional laboratory experiences, one would expect such programs to become increasingly significant.

9. *The internship.* The role which the internship will play in teacher education remains to be decided. Although it has been discussed earlier, it would seem derelict not to include this development in any presentation of issues and trends. The potential inherent in the internship concept has yet to be fully realized; but there seems to be little doubt but that it will remain on the educational scene and, in all probability, will grow in popularity. The increasing enrollments in public schools and the corresponding demand for teachers appear to be the principal deterrent to its further spread at present since it takes an extra year of college in most programs. The five-year teacher education program, including the internship, is inevitable as the complexities of teaching continue to multiply.

[1] W. R. Fulton and O. J. Rupiper, "Observation of Teaching: Direct vs. Vicarious Experiences," The Journal of Teacher Education, June, 1962, pp. 157-164.

10. *The emphasis in teacher education.* Teacher educators are becoming increasingly aware of aspects of teacher education which were not apparent a few years ago. Among these is the preparation of teachers for more specialized duties. Urban colleges are involved at present with programs preparing teachers to teach underprivileged and culturally deprived pupils. In the Southwest and in Southern California as well as in large metropolitan areas, attention is being given to teaching pupils to whom English is not a native language, particularly Spanish-speaking Americans.

Closely allied to this area is the increased concern for the impetus of mental health in education. Interest is evident in improving the mental health of teachers in preparation as well as in educating them to improve the mental health of pupils who will be in their charge.

Another changing emphasis in teacher education programs is the inclusion of some form of preparation for team-teaching and the use of the new educational developments, *i.e.*, television, programmed learning, independent study, etc. It should be recognized that the movement toward including these areas in teacher education programs is not as significant as might be desired; however, progress is slowly being made. Within a few years, teacher education programs must, of necessity, include these aspects of teaching if public schools are to keep up with modern society. There are scattered student teaching programs involving team teaching assignments and also some utilization of televised instruction.

It seems apparent to those involved in teacher education that there will always be some issues to be resolved. It is also noticeable that progress is made from these very issues. Teacher education, which has improved markedly during the past decade, will undoubtedly continue its improvement; and progress during the next decade may well be remarkable. The increasing interest of the academic community which formerly looked with jaundiced eye toward teacher education can well be the support for such improvement as teacher educators and academicians work together for the general upgrading of the effort. The increasing support evidenced by the federal government in improving teacher education also provides strength to teacher educators who desire to move ahead. The combination of these factors is finally bringing teacher education to the professional level which it has sought for many years. Such a result "is a supposition devoutly to be wished."

ADDITIONAL REFERENCES

Caswell, Hollis L., "The Education of Teachers in the Sixties," *Childhood Education*, 40:447-451, May, 1964.

__________, "The Influence of Developments in Higher Education on Teacher Preparation," *The Journal of Teacher Education*, 14:206-211, June, 1963.

Chase, Francis S., "Teacher Education for the Next Decade," *School and Society*, 92:140-142, March 21, 1964.

Gudridge, Beatrice M., "Axioms and Issues in Teacher Education," *Minnesota Journal of Education*, 44:8-9, January, 1964.

Nash, Curtis and Yvonne Lofthouse, *New Developments, Research, and Experimentation in Professional Laboratory Experiences*, Bulletin No. 22, The Association for Student Teaching, 1964.

Ornstein, Allan C., "Teacher Training for 'Difficult Schools'", *Journal of Secondary Education*, 39:172-173, April, 1964.

Schunk, Bernadene, *The Outlook in Student Teaching*, 41st Yearbook, The Association for Student Teaching, 1962, pp. 159-168.

Steeves, Frank L., *Issues in Student Teaching*, New York: The Odyssey Press, 1963.

Wilhelms, Fred, "Exploring New Paths in Teacher Education," *Theory Into Practice*, 3:12-16, February, 1964.

Appendix

A Recommended Professional Library for the Cooperating School

Association for Student Teaching Yearbooks (since 1956):

Four Went to Teach, Dorothy M. McGeoch (Editor), 35th Yearbook, 1956.

Guidance in Teacher Education, Herbert J. Klausmeier (Editor), 36th Yearbook, 1957.

Improving Instruction in Professional Education, Clyde I. Martin (Editor), 37th Yearbook, 1958.

The Supervising Teacher, Ernest J. Milner (Editor), 38th Yearbook, 1959.

Evaluating Student Teaching, Andrew D. Rippey (Editor), 39th Yearbook, 1960.

Teacher Education and the Public Schools, Charles M. Clarke (Editor), 40th Yearbook, 1961.

The Outlook in Student Teaching, Bernadene Schunk (Editor), 41st Yearbook, 1962.

Concern for the Individual in Student Teaching, Ted Ward (Editor), 42nd Yearbook, 1963.

The College Supervisor--Conflict and Challenge, Robert Pfeiffer (Editor), 43rd Yearbook, 1964.

Association for Student Teaching Bulletins:

Number 1, *Guiding Student Teaching Experiences,* 1951.

Number 2, *Helping Student Teachers Through Evaluation,* 1953.

Number 3, *Helping Student Teachers Through Conferences,* 1954.

Number 4, *Helping Student Teachers Work with Parents,* 1955.

Number 5, *Helping Student Teachers Assume Responsibility,* 1956.

Number 6, *Encouraging Creativity in Student Teaching,* 1956.

Number 7, *Prospective Teachers Learn from Experiences with Children and Youth,* 1957.

Number 8, *Achieving Quality in Off-Campus Professional Laboratory Experiences*, 1957.
Number 9, *The Purposes, Functions, and Uniqueness of the College-Controlled Laboratory School*, 1958.
Number 10, *Helping Student Teachers Understand and Utilize Consultant Services*, 1959.
Number 11, *A Guide to Planning for Off-Campus Student Teaching*, 1959.
Number 12, *Preparation for Cooperative Decision Making*, 1960.
Number 13, *Student Teaching: A Mission of the Elementary and Secondary Schools*, 1960.
Number 14, *A Case Study of a Workshop*, 1960.
Number 15, *The Value Approach to Student Teaching*, 1960.
Number 16, *Building Good Relationships: A Major Role of the College Supervisor*, 1961.
Number 17, *The Relation of Theory to Practice inEducation*, 1962.
Number 18, *Case Studies in Student Teaching*, 1962.
Number 19, *The Student Teacher Evaluates Pupil Progress*, 1962.
Number 20, *Research and Professional Experiences in Teacher Education*, 1963.
Number 21, *The Student Teacher's Experiences in the Community*, 1964.
Number 22, *New Developments, Research, and Experimentation in Professional Laboratory Experiences*, 1964.
Number 23, *The Student Teacher: Managing an Elementary Classroom*, 1964.

Professional Books:

Andrews, Leonard O., *Student Teaching*, The Center for Applied Research in Education, Inc., New York, 1964.

Brown, Thomas J., *Student Teaching in a Secondary School*, Harper and Brothers, New York, 1960. (Contains appendix for cooperating teacher).

Brown, Thomas J. and Serafina F. Banich, *Student Teaching in an Elementary School*, Harper and Brothers, New York, 1962. (Contains appendix for cooperating teacher).

Curtis, Dwight K. and Leonard O. Andrews, *Guiding Your Student Teacher*, Prentice-Hall, Englewood Cliffs, N. J., 1954.

Greene, Gwynn A., *Problem Situations in Student Teaching*, Bureau of Publications, Teachers College, Columbia University, New York, 1959.

Haines, Aleyne C., *Guiding the Student Teaching Process in Elementary Education*, Rand McNally and Company, Chicago, 1960.

Hunter, Elizabeth, *The Cooperating Teacher at Work; Case Studies of Critical Incidents*, Bureau of Publications, Teachers College, Columbia University, New York, 1962.

Milner, Ernest J., *You and Your Student Teacher*, Bureau of Publications, Teachers College, Columbia University, New York, 1954.

Steeves, Frank L,, *Issues in Student Teaching*, Odyssey Press, Inc., New York, 1963.

Stratemeyer, Florence B. and Margaret Lindsey, *Working with Student Teachers*, Bureau of Publications, Teachers College, Columbia University, New York, 1958.

Professional Journals:

The Journal of Teacher Education, published quarterly by the National Commission on Teacher Education and Professional Standards, National Education Association.

Index